Veritatis Splendor Thirty Years Later
Pastoral Insights

Edited by
James Keating

En Route Books and Media, LLC
Saint Louis, MO

⊛ENROUTE
Make the time

5705 Rhodes Avenue
Saint Louis, MO 63109

Copyright 2024 and 2026 James Keating

All Rights Reserved. No part of this book may be reproduced, stored in a retrieval system, or transmitted by any means, electronic, mechanical, photocopying, recording, or otherwise, without the written permission of the Institute for Priestly Formation.

ISBN-13: 979-8-88870-504-9
Library of Congress Control Number:
Available online at https://catalog.loc.gov

Scripture texts in this work are taken from the New American Bible, revised edition © 2010, 1991, 1986, 1970 Confraternity of Christian Doctrine, Washington, D.C. and are used by permission of the copyright owner. All Rights Reserved. No part of the New American Bible may be reproduced in any form without permission in writing from the copyright owner.

Cover image: Stained glass window with the image of Pope Saint John Paul II in the window of the church, the shrine of Our Lady in Chełm, Poland. Design by Timothy D. Boatright.

Contributors

Justin M. Anderson, PhD, is Professor and Chair of Moral Theology at Immaculate Conception Seminary School of Theology at Seton Hall University in South Orange, New Jersey.

Father Thomas Berg, PhD, is Professor of Moral Theology at Saint Joseph's Seminary and College in Yonkers, New York.

Father Dennis J. Billy, CSsR, STD, DMin, is Professor and the Robert F. Leavitt Distinguished Service Chair of Theology at St. Mary's Seminary and University in Baltimore, Maryland.

Bishop Earl K. Fernandes, PhD, STL, is Bishop of Columbus, Ohio and former Academic Dean at Mount Saint Mary's Seminary in Cincinnati, Ohio.

Beth A. Rath, PhD, is Associate Professor of Philosophy at Borromeo Seminary Institute at John Carroll University in Cleveland, Ohio.

Table of Contents

Introduction 1

Truth, Objective Morality, and Conversion
Justin M. Anderson 5

Veritatis Splendor and Intrinsic Evil
Beth A. Rath 23

Formation of Conscience in Veritatis Splendor
Dennis J. Billy, CSsR 45

*Veritatis Splendor and Pastoral Accompaniment:
Diakonia Veritatis and the Art of Speaking the Truth in Love*
Thomas Berg 71

Veritatis Splendor: A Bishop's Response
Earl K. Fernandes 91

Introduction

Veritatis Splendor caused quite a stir in the theological world when it appeared thirty years ago. The lightning rod that attracted so much attention was John Paul II's insistence on the reality of intrinsically evil acts.[1] He argued that there are such acts whose object admits no lessening of its evil, regardless of circumstances. Some freely chosen human acts are simply wrong in themselves. The preponderance of these acts gathers around the experiences of life and death, and sexual acts. At least, those are the areas that many theologians wanted to address in their dissent from the encyclical.

Thirty years later, voices still wish to find ways to lessen the gravity of these acts categorized as intrinsically evil. They are not content to allow circumstances to mitigate the level of responsibility imputed to the agent; they want circumstances to enter the object of the act itself and relieve the agent of sin. John Paul II was aware of the reality of such dissent. He knew that many sought to relieve people from the exacting nature of moral living, but he stood firm. One way to understand why he stood firm was to see how he contextualized moral living within the larger ambit of communion with Christ. Fidelity to moral living was not restricted to the individual will of persons, but the very life and love of Christ was offered to help secure one's movement from sin to virtue.

In Jesus's own day, people realized that participating in Christ's way of living moral goodness would entail suffering: "This saying is hard; who can accept it?" (Jn 6:60). After receiving this question from His disciples, Jesus immediately began to talk about the supernatural, the spiritual life. John Paul II also knew that only if one participated in the supernatural would he refrain from rationalizing the goodness of immoral acts that yield pleasure and participate in the Cross. We can be faithful to such moral demands only *in Christ*. We can assent to living a chaste life, we can embrace suffering and sickness without recourse to euthanasia, we can see possibilities that offer themselves besides choosing abortion *only* if we are in companionship with Christ. Our weakened wills and darkened minds tend toward self-interest not holiness. Holiness is given as a share in the life of God, and sharing in the life of God enables us to choose the good despite suffering. The gift of *Veritatis Splendor* is the gift of encouraging Catholics to remain in communion with Christ through the sacramental life and the life of prayer while embracing the cross of moral conversion.

Such a life is normally accessed at the parish level. All the supernatural aids to choose the good, the true, and the holy are located within the parish and its sacramental and communal realities. The essays in this book, originating at a symposium sponsored by Kenrick-Glennon Seminary in 2023, assist the pastor to instantiate *Veritatis Splendor* in his parish and to call his own people to a morality that is not a matter only of "disposing oneself to hear a teaching and obediently accepting a commandment. More radically, it involves *holding fast to the very person of Jesus*, partaking of his life and his destiny, sharing in his free and loving obedience to the will of the Father."[2]

Deacon James Keating, PhD
Former General Editor, IPF Publications
Professor, Kenrick-Glennon Seminary
St. Louis, Missouri

Notes

1. See, for example, Michael E. Allsopp and John J. O'Keefe, eds., *Veritatis Splendor: American Responses* (Kansas City: Sheed and Ward, 1995).
2. John Paul II, *Veritatis Splendor* (1993), sec. 19.

Truth, Objective Morality, and Conversion

Justin M. Anderson

"One word of truth shall outweigh the whole world."
Alexandr Solzhenitsyn[1]

Beginning from Today's Implicit Ethic

A general message of our Holy Father, Pope Francis, is that as disciples of Christ, we need to attend with greater care to those to whom we are speaking. For theologians, in particular, this means that eschewing engagement "with the world of cultures and sciences" leads theology to forget the evangelizing aspect of its mission as one becomes "content with a desk-bound theology."[2] Breaking away from the desk by attending to other sciences and human experience is ultimately to aid "our discernment on how best to bring the Gospel message to different cultural contexts and groups."[3]

We begin, then, not by listening to our own voice on ethics but by listening to that of the implicit ethic in today's Western world. Some have dismissed that Occidental modern lifestyle as nothing more than hedonism. However, philosopher Charles Taylor argues that this brush-aside maneuver tends to miss the moral impetus to which the modern secular person feels himself or herself bound.[4] Instead, Taylor discerns that we live in an age with its own ethical forces, best described as an ethic of authenticity to oneself. Without the meaning-giving structures of bygone ages, the modern individual cannot help but be launched on a lifelong quest to "find oneself." The search's only deadly foe is inauthenticity, permitting something else to impose a definition of oneself or one's own way of being human. Peter Berger noted the same thing decades before. "Put differently, there is a built-in identity crisis in the contemporary situation."[5] The individual, therefore, traverses life looking to discover and then live out his or her own way of being human, his or her own authentic self, hidden away from anyone else.

So, for scholars like Taylor, there exists an ethical ideal people live for, and it is not merely for the sake of pleasure. Nevertheless, if Taylor is correct, then there is a consequent moral relativism. This moral relativism does not come about because the modern world is reading relativistic, ethical philosophers. Instead, it is a relativism that naturally follows from a radical individualism that foresees each person bearing the ". . . right to develop their own form of life, grounded in their own sense of what is really important or of value. . . . What this consists of, each must, in the last instance, determine for him- or herself. No one else can or should try to dictate its content."[6] In short, a radical individualism leads to an ethics of authenticity, and an ethics of authenticity leads to a "dictatorial nature of relativism."[7] Everyone must be free to determine what is meaningful, valuable, and significant for human life. Each must do this on his or her own, finding his or her own meaning, value, and what counts as significant for them. Anyone who attempts to hold forth an objective standard is harming the quest for authenticity of those around them.[8]

However, this modern ethic is, in Taylor's words, ultimately "self-stultifying" and, in fact, "destroy[s] the conditions for realizing authenticity itself."[9] Taylor thinks this because the relativistic search for authenticity can never successfully eliminate the need for some external measure. While this relativism proposes that "things have significance not of themselves but because people deem them to have it," Taylor thinks this misses the fact we can propose individual significance only against a wider backdrop of human significance.[10] He writes, "I may be the only person with exactly 3,732 hairs on my head, or be exactly the same height as some tree on the Siberian plain, but so what?"[11] We recognize that these are not properties that have any human significance, and our personal feelings or decisions that they are significant properties cannot make them such. He concludes that "one of the things we can't do, if we are to define ourselves significantly, is suppress or deny the horizons against which things take on significance for us."[12] For Taylor, there exist inescapable horizons of meaning and significance.

From within the Catholic intellectual tradition, we might find in the rationale of Thomas Aquinas another misgiving raised against the modern ethic of authenticity in its most radical form. Concerning God's law as the measure of human life, Aquinas wrote, "there is no man or angel whose will does not need to be ruled and directed by divine law. Hence, *it is impossible* for any man not to be subject to God's precepts."[13] The strength of Aquinas's statement is striking. He does not say "one should not" or "few can accomplish such a feat." He states: "*impossibile est.*"

Aquinas might reason as follows. The human will *is* the rational appetite.[14] That is, the will *is* the desiring evoked following upon the mind's grasping. So, Aquinas might reason, by its very nature, the human will is a desire, something moving beyond itself toward what it takes to be a desirable object. This desirable object—whether an action, a material product, or even a simple thought—becomes the will's end, the desire's aim. This object becomes the person's purpose, significance, or meaning for any action that proceeds from that desire. All of this is wrapped up into what the will of its nature is. Precisely because of this relationship, the desired object necessarily acts as a measure upon the desire. "Human actions . . . have a measure of goodness from the end on which they depend."[15] This all forces us to draw the surprising conclusion that the will, in desiring some object, renders itself, in some sense, subservient to that object's gravitational pull. That desirable object, for which the person freely bends in thought and act, is necessarily transformed into a standard, or measure, of the person's striving. If one aims to act fairly toward one's coworkers, then the standard against which one's actions are measured is necessarily the fairness owed to one's coworkers. This standard taken up by the will is not imposed upon the will from some external force, yet it does constitute an external measure. Instead, it is necessarily and naturally taken up by the person the moment he or she rationally desires anything. The human will, because it is a rational appetite, necessarily has a measure it will serve.

Aquinas goes on to argue that any measure eventually must fall back to be measured by God's own self. But already, Aquinas, like Taylor, can present a rationale for why the moral relativism of today's ethic of authenticity ultimately "self-destructs."[16]

Their arguments do differ in, perhaps, important respects. Nevertheless, both authors acknowledge not only the "givenness" of the good or significance, but also that human volition cannot function in any other way.

Our First Conversion: Turning toward the Truth of Things

One who acknowledges that the existence of some measure of goodness, meaning, and significance for human life lies outside the human agent himself has already experienced what I call our first conversion. Our first conversion lies in turning outside of ourselves for the standard of what counts for a good life, a life full of real meaning and significance. The account of the rich young man in Mark's Gospel catches this seeking outside oneself in a telling way: "a man ran up, knelt down before him, and asked him" (Mk 10:17). The description of the rich young man's approach to Christ underscores that to declare ourselves in need of a standard of goodness outside of our own wishes means we must declare ourselves learners. If we could use Latin to describe this state of being a learner, we would hear ourselves admitting we are "disciples" [*discipulus*]. But what are we setting ourselves to learn, and from whom shall we learn it?

In the context we have been speaking, we wish to be disciples of what is authentically good, meaningful, and significant for human life: "Teacher, what good must I do to gain eternal life?" (Mt 19:16) Aiming to know this and recognizing it as a standard that can measure one's life is, in the end, the recognition of an "objective morality."[17] In this context, then, "objective morality" means acknowledging that there is a standard or measure for what is really good, meaningful, or significant, and we wish to learn this and follow it. In short, we wish to know the truth of things:

Jesus, as a patient and sensitive teacher, answers the young man by taking him, as it were, by the hand, and leading him step by step to the full truth.[18]

Truth can be defined in many ways. The most common definition heard in the Catholic intellectual tradition is that "truth is a conformity between reality and the mind [*veritas est adaequatio rei et intellectus*]."[19] This is a healthy notion of truth that comes from Aristotle, and its main function is to link what we know in our minds to reality outside of our minds. So, my idea of a cypress tree is true when it matches the real-world existence of a cypress tree. However, this way of thinking about truth has a limit: it explains truth only in the mind. It explains how one's *ideas* are "true": they are correctly conformed to reality.

Also present in the Catholic intellectual tradition is another, sometimes neglected, definition of truth, one that comes from Augustine of Hippo through Anselm of Canterbury. This notion of truth speaks not to truth in the mind, but truth when created realities are in conformity with the Divine Mind. This idea is truth as rectitude or rightness. In this sense, "something is called true when it conforms to the Divine Mind [*adaequationem ad intellectum divinum dicitur vera*]."[20] In this manner of speaking of the truth, we can say that "She is a true Catholic" or "He is a true priest." It is this oft-neglected understanding of truth that immediately implies some standard or measure. Only here the standard of rightness is clear: it is the Divine Mind. This definition of truth explains how *things* are "true": they are correctly conformed to the Divine Mind's creative plan for them.

Springing forth from the latter understanding of truth are three notes. The first is that we are seeking not only what a thing is, but what it is meant to be. Indeed, within this notion of truth is hidden the authenticity of that very thing. Here, we find the foundation for a Christian and humanly healthy notion of authenticity.

This leads to the second point. The "real" or "true" version of some thing is what it is meant to be. But this best version of it is necessarily determined, not by our wishes and whims, but by the Divine Mind. It is the divine idea of the created reality that ultimately measures its authenticity. The creating Divine Mind is recognized as the standard of authenticity for every created reality. From this perspective, we can affirm with the great Catholic minds of the Middle Ages that all of reality is that which exists between two minds: the divine creative Thinker and the receptive human mind. And this understanding of truth as rectitude underscores the full weight of our confession of God as Creator. As the Catechism states, "Catechesis on creation is of major importance. It concerns the very foundations of human and Christian life."[21]

In a third and final note, we cannot ignore the *moral* implication of this notion of truth as conformity to the Divine Mind. It is namely this: that the rightness of our lives is measured according to the divine rightness. Another word for this "rightness" or "rectitude" is righteousness. Thus, the ultimate measure of all righteousness is what the Catholic intellectual tradition has, since the time of Augustine of Hippo, called "Eternal Law." We arrive back at what was affirmed above, namely, that *impossibile est* for the human will, for human life, not to be measured.

These three points flow one from the other so that we can now summarize them in a single statement: the unavoidable consequence of confessing the existence of a benevolent Creator is an objective, ultimate standard of morality. While this is certainly true, such an emphasis on truth can sound speculative, intimidating, even cold and harsh to modern ears. Here, it may be particularly helpful to recall that Scripture, the saints, and the mystics each reveal the bridge between the idea of reality-as-truth and other ideas such as beauty and goodness.

Claritas: From the Way of Truth to the Way of Beauty

The contemporary world does not read, never mind follow, such speculative conclusions on the nature of truth. Nevertheless, something can help us here still. It is worth noting that the bridge between truth, as we have been discussing it, and beauty lies in a quality associated with both: *claritas*. What lies behind this Latin term is something more than the modern English word "clarity" convenes. *Claritas* betrays not only clarity but brightness, radiance, refulgence, or splendor. Thus, we can say that the realities that are truest pulse with a radiance, with a particular *claritas*. Like viewing unpolluted water or unclouded skies, one does not only see things with *claritas*, but sees into them. Perhaps even more striking, true (authentic) people shine with their own radiance. A Saint Theresa of Calcutta is a splendid example of this. The wrinkled face of that short Albanian nun had its own refulgence. This is so because reality shines.

Indeed, because the real possesses a *claritas*, it grounds the instinctual acknowledgement that there comes to the mind a light that illuminates. We speak of a moment of epiphany as "seeing the light." When a cartoonist wishes to illustrate a character having an idea, an insight, the cartoonist draws a light bulb above the character's head. Gerald Phelan notes that Aquinas also shared this instinctual association between light and intelligibility. Phelan writes, "*claritas* is in the realm of intelligibility and truth; it expresses most aptly the power of reality to reveal itself to the mind."[22]

The Dutch philosopher Jan Aertsen indicates its role of making things visible:

> For clarity is identified by Thomas with truth and the knowability of things. It is described as light. The mark of light, both physical and spiritual, is that it makes things visible.[23]

While truth and intelligibility are tied to this *claritas* of reality, *claritas* has long been held to be a fundamental property of something else: beauty. Thomas Aquinas lists *claritas* as one of the three constitutive elements for beauty to exist:

> For beauty includes three things: *integritas* or "perfection," since those things which are impaired are by the very fact ugly; due *proportio* or "harmony"; and lastly, *claritas* or "splendor", from which things are called beautiful.[24]

A being that possesses *claritas* does two things simultaneously. First, it clarifies, rendering itself intelligible, capable of making itself understandable. Second, it radiates, manifesting its beauty. The encyclical *Veritatis Splendor* is, as it were, describing the true beauty. "The splendor of truth shines forth in all the works of the Creator."[25]

Just as there was an implicit ethical dimension to all we said about the truth of things from the Creator, so too is there the same dimension with *claritas* as the way of beauty. For just as when things are most truly themselves—which is to say "as the Creator fashioned them to be"—they radiate, so too they manifest a captivating splendor. What shines here is the *claritas* of the Divine. Therefore, addressing the moral dimension, it is more proper to say it is a divine radiance shining through a well-lived human life. And even, perhaps, before a particular human life shines with such a moral radiance, the desire to be touched by such clarifying radiance is within us. As the psalmist writes, "Lord, show us the light of your face!" (Ps 4:6) Of course, that which is most perfect, which is most completely in accord with God's call, shines forth all the more. It is this moral dimension, this divine radiance particularly and uniquely manifest in each life diversely, that is most especially "the splendor of truth."[26] Beauty is the radiance of the true good. But from what font does this radiance of life come?

Our Second Conversion: Christ, the Claritas of the Father

Above, while exploring the relation of truth to *claritas*, we encountered Gerald Phelan's passage regarding *claritas*'s link to intelligibility. Now we are better suited to give the full passage with all of its Christological force. Phelan writes,

> *claritas* is in the realm of intelligibility and truth; it expresses most aptly the power of reality to reveal itself to the mind. Thus, St. Thomas does not hesitate to say that the Second Person of the Blessed Trinity is the Eternal Light of the Father because He is the Truth of God, the *Verbum*—"Insofar as he is the Father's perfect Word, he has the *claritas* that radiates over all things and in which all things shine forth." It is from this Source that the rays of divine splendor stream into finite things, flooding them with beauty.[27]

Christ, the Truth of God, radiates most completely and most perfectly that Divine Light. Nor is this a surprise. What else is meant by the fundamental teaching for every Christian that Christ is the fullness of God's revelation? It is on the countenance of Christ, the perfect Word of the Father, that one sees God most clearly.

Notice, we are not making a mere pious declamation about what Christ came to do, about His divine task on earth. We are affirming who He is. Scripture also attests to this identity of Christ. Paul speaks of Christ as "the image of the invisible God" (Col 1:15). The Gospel of John recounts Christ's own words to His apostles when Philip asks Him to "show us the Father" (Jn 14:8). "Have I been with you for so long a time and you still do not know me, Philip? Whoever has seen me has seen the Father" (Jn 14:9). More pointedly still, the author of the Letter to the Hebrews writes of Christ that He is "the refulgence of his [God's] glory" (Heb 1:3).

So, Christ is the refulgence or *claritas* of the Father. It is His undiminished splendor that shines over all creatures, flooding them with their own beauty. "All things came to be through him, and without him nothing came to be" (Jn 1:3-4). The single and unique *claritas* of the Word becomes the cause of all other refulgence in created beings. "God gives to all creatures, through a certain refulgence, the handing down of His radiant luminous ray . . . and that handing down renders one beautiful, that is makes beauty in things."[28] Thus, any refulgence that a human life might possess is, whether through grace or nature, a gift from Christ. And in this way, "the beauty of creatures is nothing other than a likeness of participated beings to the divine beauty."[29]

For one who acknowledges Christ as the Word of God, then, Christ becomes both the place of encounter with God and the recognized source of the light one needs, and for which one looks. The opening words of *Veritatis Splendor* remind us of both these aspects of Christ:

> The light of God's face shines in all its beauty on the countenance of Jesus Christ. . . .Consequently the decisive answer to every one of man's questions, his religious and moral questions in particular, is given by Jesus Christ, or rather is Jesus Christ himself, as the Second Vatican Council recalls: "In fact, *it is only in the mystery of the Word incarnate that light is shed on the mystery of man.*"[30]

Thus, coming to this acknowledgment, namely that Christ is the source of this refulgence, the font of our glory, constitutes at least the beginning of our second conversion. We at least turn to seek the answers to our own identity or our own journey to authenticity face to face with the countenance of the One who is the *Claritas Patris*, the refulgence of the Father.

Speaking of Christ in this way unlocks for us the way of beauty, a way Pope Francis has indicated as fruitful:

> Every form of catechesis would do well to attend to the "way of beauty" (*via pulchritudinis*). Proclaiming Christ means showing that to believe in and to follow him is not only something right and true, but also something beautiful.[31]

Nor is his perspective unique. It is often beauty that draws one to Christ. Basil of Caesarea writes of the attraction,

> It is natural for us to want things that are good and pleasing to the eye, even though at first different things seem beautiful and good to different people. . . . What, I ask, is

more wonderful than the beauty of God? What thought is more pleasing and wonderful than God's majesty? The radiance of divine beauty is altogether beyond the power of words to describe.[32]

John Paul II discerned the same draw present in the passage of the rich young man:

> If he asks Jesus this question, we can presume that it is not because he is ignorant of the answer contained in the Law. It is more likely that the attractiveness of the person of Jesus had prompted within him new questions about moral good. He feels the need to draw near.[33]

This spiritual magnetism is equally true today and exemplified in the short story by Flannery O'Connor entitled "Parker's Back." In that tale, we meet a wayward middle-aged man named Parker. Parker is captivated by a man at a carnival covered in tattoos. While Parker travels the world filling his entire body with tattoos, he remains somehow prescient that his back is to be saved for something special. Parker never tattoos his back. After a sudden and disorienting accident on an overturned tractor (and a burning ancient tree), Parker flees the scene into the local town. There, somewhat drunk, he feels drawn to the tattoo parlor at closing time. He can feel that the time has come to tattoo his back. Here is the scene in O'Connor's own words:

> Parker sat down with the book and wet his thumb. He began to go through it, beginning at the back where the up-to-date pictures were. Some of them he recognized—The Good Shepherd, Forbid Them Not, The Smiling Jesus, Jesus the Physician's Friend, but he kept turning rapidly backwards and the pictures became less and less reassuring.

One showed a gaunt green dead face streaked with blood. One was yellow with sagging purple eyes. Parker's heart began to beat faster and faster until it appeared to be roaring inside him like a great generator. He flipped the pages quickly, feeling that when he reached the one ordained, a sign would come. He continued to flip through until he had almost reached the front of the book. On one of the pages a pair of eyes glanced at him swiftly. Parker sped on, then stopped. His heart too appeared to cut off; there was absolute silence. It said as plainly as if silence were a language itself, GO BACK. Parker returned to the picture—the haloed head of a flat stern Byzantine Christ with all-demanding eyes. He sat there trembling; his heart began slowly to beat again as if it were being brought to life by a subtle power.

"You found what you want?" the artist asked.

Parker's throat was too dry to speak. He got up and thrust the book at the artist, opened at the picture.

"That'll cost you plenty," the artist said. "You don't want all those little blocks though, just the outline and some better features."

"Just like it is," Parker said, "just like it is or nothing."[34]

O'Connor's "Parker's Back" exemplifies various aspects of what we have been exploring. But the prose of a short story itself is an appeal to the way of beauty. This appeal is capable of not only informing but also stirring up love. Insofar as it is beautiful, it occasions a chance to glimpse Christ. Yet, the way of beauty is more than that. It would be a mistake to regard it as merely a vague appeal for aesthetical trimmings. *Evangelii Gaudium* warns that "if this invitation [to respond to the God of love] does not radiate forcefully and attractively, the edifice of the Church's moral teaching risks becoming a house of cards, and this is our greatest risk."[35] And while, for the contemporary man, a theological publication is less likely to stir in its observer an encounter with Christ, perhaps through other experiences of beauty, it very well may.[36] Regardless of the medium, like Parker, like the rich young man in the Gospel, we can say it is those eyes, those all-demanding, captivating eyes that bid us to "come, follow me" (Mt 19:21).

Notes

1. Alexandr Solzhenitsyn recounts this Russian proverb. See Alexandr Solzhenitsyn, "Noble Lecture," in *Nobel Lectures, Literature 1968–1980*, ed. Tore Frängsmyr and Sture Allén (Singapore: World Scientific Publishing, 1993).
2. Francis, *Evangelii Gaudium* (2013), sec. 133. Pope Francis also writes in the Encyclical Letter *Laudato Si'*, "Theological and philosophical reflections on the situation of humanity and the world can sound tiresome and abstract, unless they are grounded in a fresh analysis of our present situation, which is in many ways unprecedented in the history of humanity," sec. 17; See, too, Pope Francis's Letter to the General of the Redemptorists, March 23, 2021.
3. *Evangelii Gaudium*, sec. 133.
4. Taylor fingers Alan Bloom as being one example of missing the modern moral ideal at work in people. Taylor writes, "I think the relativism widely espoused today is a profound mistake, even in some respects self-stultifying. . . . [Bloom] doesn't seem to recognize that there is a powerful moral ideal at work here, however debased and travestied its expression might be. The moral ideal behind self-fulfillment is that of being true to oneself [authenticity]." Charles Taylor, *The Ethics of Authenticity* (Cambridge: Harvard University Press, 1991), 15.
5. Peter Berger, "On the Obsolescence of the Concept of Honor" in *Revisions: Changing Perspectives in Moral Philosophy*, ed. Stanley Hauerwas and Alasdair MacIntyre (Notre Dame: University of Notre Dame Press, 1983), 178. [Originally published: *European Journal of Sociology/Archives Européennes de Sociologie/Europäisches Archiv für Soziologie* 11:2, *La foi et les mœurs or Faith and Morals* (1970), 339–347.]
6. Taylor, *The Ethics of Authenticity*, 14.
7. Joseph Cardinal Ratzinger, "Homily at the Mass 'Pro Eligendo Romano Pontifice'" Vatican Basilica, April 18, 2005. Then-Cardinal Ratzinger immediately invoked the notion of an objective measure of what it means to be human: Christ. He said, "We, however, have a different goal: the Son of God, the true man. He is the measure of true humanism." Also see Joseph Cardinal Ratzinger and Marcello Pera, *Without Roots: The West, Relativism, Christianity, Islam*, trans. Michael F. Moore (New York: Basic Books, 2006), 128.
8. Pope Francis quotes with approval the U.S. bishops who highlight the presence of a "moral relativism that is joined, not without inconsistency, to a belief in the absolute rights of individuals. In this view, the Church is perceived as promoting a particular prejudice and as interfering with individual freedom." Francis, *Evangelii Gaudium*, sec. 64.
9. Taylor, *The Ethics of Authenticity*, 15 and 35, respectively.

10. Taylor, *The Ethics of Authenticity*, 36.
11. Taylor, *The Ethics of Authenticity*, 35.
12. Taylor, *The Ethics of Authenticity*, 37.
13. "Nullus autem homo est, nec etiam Angelus, cuius voluntatem non oporteat regulari et dirigi lege divina. Unde impossibile est aliquem hominem praeceptis Dei non subdi." Thomas Aquinas, *Super Epistolas S. Pauli lectura, t. 1: Super secundam Epistolam ad Corinthios lectura*, ed. R. Cai, 8th ed. (Taurini-Romae: Marietti, 1953): c. 3, lect. 3, n. 112, emphasis added.
14. Thomas Aquinas, *Summae Theologiae* in *Opera omnia iussu impensaque Leonis XIII P. M. edita, t. 4–12* (Romae: S. C. de Propaganda Fide, 1888-1906): I q. 59, a. 1; I–II q. 8, a. 1.
15. Aquinas, *Summae Theologiae* I–II q. 18, a. 4, c.
16. Taylor, *The Ethics of Authenticity*, 37.
17. This entails no repudiation or rejection of the thesis that important aspects of our ethical lives are deeply subjective and relative to each person. For example, as Aristotle noted long ago, the moral virtues are relative to each person, just as eating "too much" or "too little" is necessarily relative to the physical constitution of the person under question.
18. "Iesus enim, subtili quadam psychologica perspicientia, respondet quasi manu ducens adulescentem, pedetemptim, ad plenam veritatem." John Paul II, *Veritatis Splendor* (1993), sec. 8.
19. Thomas Aquinas, *Quaestiones disputatae de veritate* in *Opera omnia iussu Leonis XIII P. M. edita, t. 22, 1/2:* (Roma: Ad Sanctae Sabinae, 1970), q. 1, a. 1, c.
20. Aquinas, *Quaestiones disputatae de veritate*, q. 1, a. 2, c.
21. "Catechesis de creatione summi est momenti. Ad ipsa vitae humanae et christianae fundamenta refertur." *Catechism of the Catholic Church*, 2nd edition, revised in accordance with the official Latin text promulgated by Pope John Paul II (Vatican City: Libreria Editrice Vaticana, 1997), sec. 282.
22. Gerald Phelan, "The Concept of Beauty in St. Thomas Aquinas," in *G.B. Phelan: Selected Papers*, ed. Arthur G. Kirn (Toronto: Pontifical Institute of Medieval Studies, 1967), 155–180, at 178.
23. Jan A. Aertsen, "Beauty in the Middle Ages: A Forgotten Transcendental?" in *Medieval Philosophy and Theology* vol. 1 (1991): 68–97, at 93.
24. "Nam ad pulchritudinem tria requiruntur. Primo quidem, integritas sive perfectio, quae enim diminuta sunt, hoc ipso turpia sunt. Et debita proportio sive consonantia. Et iterum claritas, unde quae habent colorem nitidum, pulchra esse dicuntur." Aquinas, *Summae Theologiae* I–II q. 39, a. 8, c.
25. "Veritatis splendor in omnibus Creatoris operibus effulget." John Paul II, *Veritatis Splendor*, sec. 1.
26. Justin M. Anderson, "Diversity: A Catholic Understanding." *Logos: A Journal Of Catholic Thought & Culture* 25, n. 3 (2022): 27–60.

27. Phelan, "The Concept of Beauty in St. Thomas Aquinas," 178. The quote is from Aquinas's Commentary on the Sentences. See Thomas Aquinas, *Scriptum super libros Sententiarum magistri Petri Lombardi episcopi Parisiensis*, tom. 1, ed. P. Mandonnet (Paris: P. Lethielleux, 1929): I, d. 31, q. 2, a. 1, c.

28. The full passage runs: "Deus sit causa claritatis, ostendit subdens, quod Deus immittit omnibus creaturis, cum quodam fulgore, traditionem sui radii luminosi, qui est fons omnis luminis; quae quidem traditiones fulgidae divini radii, secundum participationem similitudinis sunt intelligendae et istae traditiones sunt pulchrificae, idest facientes pulchritudinem in rebus." Thomas Aquinas, *In librum Beati Dionysii De divinis nominibus expositio*, ed. C. Pea, P. Caramello, C. Mazzantini (Turin-Rome: Marietti, 1950): c. 4, lect. 5.

29. "Pulchritudo enim creaturae nihil est aliud quam similitudo divinae pulchritudinis in rebus participata." Aquinas, *De divinis nominibus*, c. 4, lect 5.

30. "Vultus Dei lumen integra sua pulchritudine super Iesu Christi vultum splendet. . . . Eam ob rem supremum responsum ad quamlibet hominis quaestionem, ad quaestiones praesertim religiosas et morales, Iesus Christus dat, immo ipse Christus est, uti Concilium Vaticanum II affirmat: "Reapse nonnisi im mysterio Verbi incarnati mysterium hominis vere clarescit." John Paul II, *Veritatis Splendor*, sec. 2.

31. *Evangelii Gaudium*, sec. 167; the paragraph cites: Vatican II, *Inter Mirifica* (1963), sec. 6;

32. Basil of Caesarea, "The Long Rules," in *Saint Basil, Aesthetical Works, Fathers of the Church: A New Translation*, ed. Roy J. Deferrari, trans. Sr. M. Monica Wagner (Washington DC: Catholic University of America Press, 1962) resp. 2 (234); here, as in "Tuesday, Office of Readings, First Week of Ordinary Time," in *The Liturgy of the Hours according to the Roman Rite* (New York: Catholic Book Publishing, Co, 1975), 59–60.

33. *Veritatis Splendor*, sec. 8.

34. Flannery O'Connor, "Parker's Back" in *The Complete Stories of Flannery O'Connor* (New York: Farrar, Straus and Giroux, 1971), 522.

35. *Evangelii Gaudium*, sec. 39.

36. This can be read, and perhaps should be read, as an indictment against most theological literature. However, that indictment cannot be leveled against all equally. Besides this, however, it could also be an indictment against the common contemporary person, so ill-disposed to read serious discussion. Most likely, it is an indictment against both. Whatever the case may be, it does not render theological discourse worthless. It only means that the theological publication will have to content itself with giving words and order to that experience upon which it reflects.

Veritatis Splendor and Intrinsic Evil

Beth A. Rath

Pope John Paul II promulgated *Veritatis Splendor* in 1993, during a time of confusion among Catholic moral theologians. Proportionalists and consequentialists within the Church, like Richard McCormick, SJ and Joseph Fuchs, SJ, were challenging the Catholic teaching that there are intrinsically evil human acts. One of the Pope's central aims in drafting the encyclical was to clarify and reaffirm the consistent teaching of the Church regarding intrinsic evils in response to these challenges.

Thirty years since the publication date of *Veritatis Splendor*, the moral confusion among Catholics, moral theologians and high-ranking clerics included, is arguably just as great, even if the sorts of errors are repackaged somewhat differently and more subtly than the ones John Paul II highlighted. Published essays and official statements from Church officials have cast doubt on the intrinsically evil nature of acts like euthanasia, contraception, and non-marital sex, while also questioning whether there are really any intrinsically evil acts at all.[1] For this reason, the encyclical's lucid philosophical and theological arguments are worth revisiting in today's moral context.

My aim in this essay is to reexamine some of the key themes of *Veritatis Splendor* that pertain to the notion of intrinsic evils. To this end, I begin by highlighting Thomistic and personalist themes that form the backdrop of the encyclical. This backdrop is the foundation of the Church's teaching on intrinsic evils. I then examine intrinsic evils themselves in light of the preceding framework. Lastly, I consider two so-called "teleological" ethical theories (teleologisms) and their attending errors.

Thomistic and Personalist Backdrop

Three key themes in Thomistic and personalist moral philosophy and theology especially bear upon what Pope John Paul II says about intrinsic evils in *Veritatis Splendor*: 1) the natural law, 2) the dignity of the human person, and 3) the structure of a moral act. I consider each of these in turn.

The Natural Law

In Part I of Chapter 2 in *Veritatis Splendor*, the Pope talks at length about the natural law. He thinks of man's moral life as a "participated theonomy," "since man's free obedience to God's law effectively implies that human reason and human will participate in God's wisdom and providence."[2] It is precisely this human participation in the Eternal Law (i.e., God's providential plan for creation) that Aquinas calls the "natural law."[3] The natural law includes fundamental principles that guide human action. For Aquinas, the natural law is distinct from human positive law, such as traffic laws and laws governing commerce. These laws are human constructs, or "measures," ideally aimed at promoting the common good. The natural law, however, is not a human construct but, rather, a participation in *God's* mind and *God's* governance. It is a *measured measuring*.[4] We can measure human conduct by the natural law, but humans do not make the rules; God does. This will be important later when we consider intrinsic evils because these are not human constructs; humans do not determine what is intrinsically evil but, rather, can *discover* what is intrinsically evil based on God's design.

Pope John Paul II gives scriptural support to this understanding of the natural law by citing Genesis 2:17: "From that tree [of knowledge of good and evil] you shall not eat; when you eat from it you shall die." The passage is a warning against usurping divine authority to become the measurer of good and evil. The autonomous conscience, untethered from God's "measures," errs in becoming the creator of law unto itself. The Pope rebukes this error in *Dominum et Vivificantem*, which he cites in section 60 of *Veritatis Splendor*:

> Conscience is not an independent and exclusive capacity to decide what is good and what is evil. Rather there is profoundly imprinted upon it a principle of obedience vis-à-vis the objective norm which establishes and conditions the correspondence of its decisions with the commands and prohibitions which are at the basis of human behaviour.[5]

Conscience, then, is a witness to the natural law, not its creator or arbiter.

Importantly, this natural law, which informs each individual conscience, is both universal and immutable.[6] It is universal, first, insofar as it applies to all human beings, for all time and across cultures. This is because the law is "inscribed in the rational nature of the person."[7] The natural law, then, applies to all human beings in virtue of their shared human nature and, therefore, their shared *telos*. Citing *Gaudium et Spes*,

John Paul II describes the human *telos* as our "divine calling and destiny," namely eternal communion with God. The natural law may be understood to be universal in a second way: Because of human beings' common rational nature, the natural law, at least in its general principles, is universally *knowable* by them.[8] Knowledge of the fundamental moral principles, then, is not exclusively for the erudite or members of a specific religious group but, rather, is possible for all people.

The natural law is immutable, or unchangeable, in the sense that nothing can be subtracted from its most general principles; something cannot be part of the law at one time and then cease to be part of the law at another time.[9] That the "good is to be done and pursued and evil avoided" is an immutable principle, as is "life is a good to be pursued."[10] Further, these principles can never be absolutely removed from the human heart; they are habitually and perpetually held by human beings.[11]

The Dignity of the Human Person

Pope John Paul II uses the word "dignity" with reference to the human person and human capacities over forty times in *Veritatis Splendor*. This concept refers to a person's fundamental worth, and it provides a link between metaphysics and morality (i.e., between what a human person is and what gives moral coloration to his or her human acts).[12] When the Pope discusses dignity, he likely has in mind the works of Max Scheler and Immanuel Kant, along with those of Aquinas. Here, I restrict my comments about dignity to the work of Thomas Aquinas.

The primary sense of dignity is rooted in personhood. "'Person' is a name of dignity," says Aquinas.[13] Drawing from the masters of his day, he considers dignity to be a distinguishing and essential property of persons.[14] This claim deserves a closer look. Why does the human person have dignity? What are the foundations, or causes, of this dignity, such that persons must be respected, honored, and never used as a mere means? What follows is a non-exhaustive list of the sources of dignity.

1. Aquinas grounds the dignity of persons in their individual subsistence and intellectual nature. For him, a person is a subsistence (i.e., an existence *by itself*).[15] A subsisting individual is not the same as a nature, since natures are universals and, as such, can be predicated of many. "Human nature," for example, can be predicated alike of Socrates, Glaucon, and Adeimantus. This means that the dignity of persons is not exclusively, or even primarily, grounded in human nature, as such. Instead, it is the *subsisting individual* human being that has dignity. Individuals are unique, unrepeatable, and incommunicable. There will never be another Socrates, and even Socrates's greatest friends could not plumb the depths of his person. The subsisting individual, then, is a primary source of dignity.

2. This subsisting individual is an individual substance of a *rational*, or *intellectual*, nature. All persons, including humans, angels, and God, have a rational nature. Because of their rational nature, persons can control their own actions.[16] They are not moved to their end by some external principle but, rather, can move themselves toward their end in virtue of intellectual knowledge of that end. Aquinas calls the acts eliciting from an internal principle such as this "voluntary acts."[17]

   Karol Wojtyla, in his philosophical writings prior to his election to the Holy See, thinks of this capacity of persons in terms of "self-determination."[18] Not only are human persons able to determine their own specific actions, but they also determine their moral character by self-directed action. This capacity for voluntary, self-determining action, which is rooted in the rational powers of intellect and will and instantiated in each individual person, is at the root of all morality. Only beings that are self-directed count as moral agents. The rational powers and capacity for moral agency, then, are sources of dignity, elevating human beings to a status above plants and other animals.

3. A third reason for our especial dignity is that human beings are created in the image of God.[19] God is a person *par excellence* (i.e., an individual substance of a rational nature), albeit exceeding all limitations found in creatures and materiality. The image of God is proper to rational creatures alone.[20] Human persons are created in God's image insofar as they are individual substances with rational natures. As such, they participate in God's intellectual dignity, even if the image is imperfect (i.e., their intellectual capacities are not equal to God's).[21]

4. A fourth reason for the dignity of the human person is that the Second Person of the Trinity took on human nature. According to the orthodox understanding of the Incarnation formulated at the Council of Chalcedon in 451, the Incarnate Second Person of the Trinity is a Divine Person with two natures, one divine and one *human*. The very fact that Jesus Christ assumed a human nature dignifies it.[22] According to Aquinas, the Incarnation also *reveals* the dignity of human nature by showing that intellectual enjoyment of God is possible for human beings; there is room in the Godhead for human nature.

The Structure of a Moral Act

A consideration of the Thomistic account of human action is important for understanding the heart of *Veritatis Splendor*, especially Chapter 2, Part IV in which Pope John Paul II discusses the moral act, intrinsic evils, and attending errors in the evaluation of moral acts.

Before examining the structure of moral acts, a word needs to be said about what count as moral acts at all. Aquinas distinguishes two types of action performed by human agents, namely, an act of man (*actus hominis*) and a properly human act (*actus humanus*).[23] Respirating, aging, and natural hair growth are examples of "acts of man." They are mere happenings in man, whether or not he is aware of them or consciously chooses them. Human acts, however, are properly *human* insofar as they involve knowledge and the will.[24] One must consciously will to donate clothing to the poor, for example; it does not happen automatically without our awareness and choice of the will, as aging does. Human acts, therefore, originate in the human will and are voluntary. They alone can be moral acts, taking on the quality of either moral goodness or evil and forming the character of the agent as either morally good or evil.[25]

Human acts can go wrong in a multitude of ways. According to Aquinas, if an act lacks the fullness of being (i.e., is deficient in goodness in any way), that act is evil.[26] Aquinas carefully distinguishes three parts, or determinants, that compose the structure of a moral act. Each of these determinants must be good (or not evil) in order for the human act to count as good.

These parts of a moral act include: 1) the moral object, 2) the end, and 3) the circumstances.[27] It is important to understand the proper meaning of each of these terms, especially since a failure here can occasion serious practical and pastoral errors.

The Moral Object

Human acts embody a choice and a command of the will, which makes the object of the act a *moral* object.[28] Since humans interact with the world through the powers of reason and will, the physical acts they choose to perform are bound up with intentionality; they have a tendency or directedness about them.[29] Aquinas calls the given direction or end (*finis/telos*) of the action done by the human agent the *finis operis*. This is the proximate end of the human agent (i.e., what he or she is doing to achieve a purpose). The *finis operis* is the moral object. To be clear, a chosen act has an end already intrinsic to it, even apart from a *further* purpose the agent may have for choosing it. The "moral object" of an action specifies the human action; it identifies what kind of human action is being performed.

The End

The fact that the moral object is the proximate *end* of the agent can muddle the distinction between the "moral object" and the "end" of the moral act, at least at first pass. Nevertheless, these determinants of a moral act are distinct. In the *De Malo*, Aquinas says that there is a double movement of the will in human acts.[30] Not only does the moral agent intend the proximate end of the act, or *finis operis*, but he also has a remote end or purpose for the sake of which he does what he does. This is the *finis operantis*, often simply referred to as the "end" of the act—the second determinant of a moral act.[31] A simple example illustrates the difference: the *finis operis* of cooking (a human act) is to make food to eat. But the *finis operantis* of the chef could be to show generous hospitality to dinner guests or to make a means by which to poison them! The *finis operantis* is the remote end, or *further end*, for which the agent is acting.

Circumstances

The third determinant of a moral act is the *circumstances*. Human acts always occur within concrete circumstances. Although Aquinas's account of circumstances contains some interpretive difficulties,[32] a strict understanding of "circumstances" refers to the accidents of a human act that fall outside the species (object) of the act.[33] Citing Cicero, Aquinas lists what count as "circumstances": "*Quis, quid, ubi, quibus auxiliis, cur, quomodo, quando*" (Who? What? Where? By which means? Why? How? and When?).[34] Picking up on the previous example of cooking, we can now add some circumstances: Cooking (moral object) outdoors over an open flame in the middle of tall, dry grass in an area surrounded by wildfires in the summer of 2023 (circumstances) in order to show hospitality to dinner guests (end).

All three of the determinants of a moral act can give the act its moral valence; they can make an act to be morally good or morally bad. Moral objects can be in and of themselves bad (i.e., intrinsically evil)—a topic explored further in the next section. An agent's remote end, the *finis operantis*, can also be good or bad; but this remote end cannot make an act with a bad moral object to be good (e.g., contracepting for the sake of freeing oneself to do mission work). The circumstances can change the moral quality of the act, too, but they cannot make an act with a bad moral object or even a bad end to be good.

They can, however, make an otherwise good act to be bad, as seen in the example above.[35]

Intrinsic Evils

Intrinsic evils, are, as Pope John Paul II says, "the central theme of . . . [the] Encyclical [*Veritatis Splendor*]."[36] The consistent teaching of the Church prohibits "always and without exception *intrinsically evil acts*."[37] These acts are "*per se* and in themselves wrong."[38] They are evil in kind, that is, on account of their moral object alone, which gives the act its species and is what the acting person freely chooses to do. Morality, then, primarily depends on the moral object.

What, then, counts as an intrinsically evil act? Citing the *Catechism of the Catholic Church*, the Pope says that there are "specific kinds of behaviour [sic] that are always wrong to choose, because *choosing them involves a disorder of the will, that is a moral evil*."[39] Some kinds of acts are intrinsically disordered because there is no way they can serve, or be ordered to, man's final end (*telos*). This end, shared by all humans, is revealed to us by Jesus Christ to be eternal communion with God. The determining factor, then, for whether some kind of act is intrinsically evil is whether it serves this end or is directly antithetical to it. In other words, we can ask of any given act whether it glorifies God and honors human dignity, including that of oneself and others.

The Pope affirms the singular importance of the moral object, as it identifies the kind of human action being performed. He writes, "The primary and decisive element for moral judgment is the object of the human act, which establishes whether it is *capable of being ordered to the good and to the ultimate end, which is God*."[40] To be clear, then, according to Catholic moral theology, no remote good intention of the agent (*finis operantis*) or particular circumstances can swamp or remove the evil of a bad moral object. The Pope, thus, goes on to say: "[C]ircumstances or intentions can never transform an act intrinsically evil by virtue of its object into an act 'subjectively' good or defensible as a choice."[41] Alasdair MacIntyre summarizes the reason for this moral "absolutism":

> If obedience to the . . . negative exceptionless precepts . . . is necessary for the achievement of a final good of this kind, is indeed partly constitutive of a life whose choices are directed towards that good as its end, then it makes no sense to ask whether some particular violation of one of those negative precepts might not be justified [as by a good intention or extenuating circumstances].[42]

So far, I have addressed, in a general way, why some human acts count as intrinsically evil. A related question pertains to what kinds of acts, in particular, are intrinsically evil and by what means human beings can know what these acts are. Drawing from *Veritatis Splendor*, I suggest the following two ways we can know what kinds of acts, in particular, are intrinsically evil.

The first way is via Divine Revelation. In the encyclical, Pope John Paul II relates the teaching on intrinsic evils to Christ Himself, who is "the Teacher, the Risen One who . . . teaches the truth about moral action."[43] In his encounter with the rich young man, recounted in Matthew 19, Jesus ties together the human *telos* with how we are to act. He says to the man, "If you wish to enter into life, *keep the commandments*."[44] The Decalogue—the Ten Commandments—sets out the parameters of a pathway to eternal life; to obey God in these ways is to remain in communion with Him (which is our *telos*).[45] In *Reconciliatio et Poenitentia*, an Apostolic Exhortation that preceded *Veritatis Splendor*, John Paul II explicitly links the doctrine of intrinsic evils to the Ten Commandments.[46]

The Decalogue reveals several kinds of acts that are intrinsically evil. The first three commandments pertain directly to humans acknowledging, reverencing, and worshipping God alone. Human acts that directly undermine the first three commandments are intrinsically evil in their moral object. For instance, there is no way to worship idols such that the act could be good; there is no *finis operantis* and no circumstances that could make idolatry morally praiseworthy. If man's end is communion with the one, true God, then worship of false gods is absolutely antithetical to that end and, thus, is intrinsically evil.

Jesus goes on to remind the rich young man of the latter seven commandments pertaining to the love of neighbor. These commandments preserve and protect "*the good* of the person, the image of God, by protecting his *goods*,"[47] like his life, property, and good name. Keeping the latter seven commandments is not only proof of one's love of neighbor but also a demonstration of love for God; to love one's neighbor is to love what God loves, namely, all persons. Thus, John Paul II says, "[G]*enuine love for God is not possible*" without love of neighbor.[48] Nevertheless, the negative Commandments (e.g., "You shall not murder") give merely the lower limit for what counts as good human activity, consistent with loving God and neighbor. Beneath this limit, the command of God is broken; human dignity is violated, and man's *telos* is undermined.

The second way to know what kinds of acts are intrinsically evil is by means of human reason. God has endowed rational persons with the ability to recognize good and evil; He gives man reason, and, because of his rationality, a participation in His Eternal Law (i.e., the natural law). In this way, human beings can, or *should*, recognize (not construct) good and evil, at least in many cases, even apart from their awareness of the Decalogue or any texts of the Bible. We can know by the light of human reason that good ought to be done and evil, avoided; and we ought to be able to recognize that life and truth, for example, are good for the human person and ought never to be directly undermined or acted against, without exception. Human persons, therefore, are able to know by their own reason that certain kinds of acts absolutely undermine human flourishing.[49] Genocide, abortion, euthanasia, and slavery are among the acts that John Paul II, citing *Gaudium et Spes*, lists as intrinsically evil; Divine Revelation is not required to know that these kinds of acts are always evil.[50] As Archbishop Charles Chaput puts it, "The law proscribes . . . [these acts] because, by their very nature, they deform the human person,"[51] and human reason is capable of recognizing this.

These two ways that man can know good and evil—via Divine Revelation and human reason—roughly track a two-fold reason for the unchanging, always-and-for-all-time nature of intrinsic evils and subsequent moral prescriptions. Intrinsic evils are evil for all people and for all times because: 1) God, the giver of the Decalogue and the natural law is unchanging. Jesus Christ, John Paul II writes, is "the same yesterday and today and for ever."[52] Therefore, God's call to worship Him and His absolute prohibitions on acts like murder remain the same for all ages. 2) Human beings—all of them and for all time—share in the same human nature. Certain kinds of acts, then, are, for all persons and times, utterly incompatible with human dignity and glorifying God, no matter whether those persons are twenty-first century Americans, thirteenth century Italians, or Jews in the Holy Land a millennium before that.

The Errors of Teleologisms

A certain *ethos* seeking to revise moral teachings had penetrated the Church leading up to the promulgation of *Veritatis Splendor*. This *ethos* threatened two key pillars of Catholic moral teaching, both of which John Paul II reaffirms in the encyclical: firstly, that some acts can be judged to be intrinsically evil just by virtue of the moral object; and secondly, that there are exceptionless moral absolutes.[53]

So-called "revisionist theologians," including McCormick and Fuchs, are those the Pope has in his mind when he critiques certain erroneous ethical theories he calls "teleologisms."[54] The problem with these ethical theories is that either the remote intention of the agent or the consequences/outcomes of the action become the sole determinant of the moral quality of the act.

Two teleologisms are noteworthy: consequentialism and proportionalism. Consequentialism, generically speaking, includes any ethical theory that determines the rightness or wrongness of a choice or action solely based on the sum of its foreseeable consequences.[55] On this view, one ought to choose the action that results in more good and less evil.

The problem with this view is that it denies the relevance of the moral object and narrows the criterion for the moral evaluation of an act to one, namely, the consequences it produces. According to John Paul II, however, a multitude of good consequences can "never transform an act intrinsically evil by virtue of its object into an act 'subjectively' good or defensible as a choice."[56] Citing Romans 3:8, he says, "[I]t is never lawful, even for the gravest reasons, to do evil that good may come of it."[57] Nevertheless, it would be erroneous to count consequences as *completely* morally irrelevant. Foreseeable consequences, indeed, often partly constitute our reasons for acting (*finis operantis*) and the circumstances of a moral act.[58] Certainly, prior to acting, an agent ought to think through possible consequences of his act (who or what might be affected, etc.) even if one can never fully foresee all the consequences of an action.[59]

Proportionalism, a second teleologism, is a more complex variant of consequentialism.[60] Two principles are important for proportionalists.[61] The first is the "Principle of Totality." This is described by Pope John Paul II in terms of a "fundamental option"; revisionist moral theologians, he says, claim that a person can make an *overall* self-determination (i.e., a fundamental option for his life) apart from any individual actions.[62] This fundamental option, or life-orientation, is what gives a person and even his individual actions their moral coloring.[63] Proportionalist theologian Joseph Fuchs, for example, employed this principle when he said that married couples may licitly contracept *individual acts* of sexual intercourse in case these acts are, *overall*, "ordered to the expression of the union of love."[64]

The problem with the Principle of Totality is that it introduces a false distinction between and, even siloing of, the fundamental option and particular actions. In reality, the two are closely bound together: one's individual actions build up one's habits and also *reveal* one's character. In this way, John Paul II rightly affirms that the "*so-called fundamental option . . . is always brought into play through conscious and free decisions.*"⁶⁵ Marriage vows of free, total, faithful, and fruitful love, for instance, are only lived out in the particular actions of the spouses, including each individual sexual act.

The second principle is the "Principle of Proportionate Good," sometimes called the "preference principle." According to this principle, the greater good is to be preferred and can justify so-called "pre-moral" evils. For instance, while contracepting may be a "pre-moral evil," it may be justified if it results in some "higher good," which is an outcome foreseen and intended by the couple.

The error here is a confusion about the moral object and intentionality. Proportionalists see the moral object as amoral, pre-moral, or morally neutral, apart from a consideration of the end, or *finis operantis*. This false way of understanding the moral object and intentionality leads to a second problem: denying moral absolutes. For proportionalists, a noble *finis operantis* can justify actions traditionally thought to be intrinsically evil in kind. Thus, acts such as abortion and euthanasia would be either morally good or bad depending on the remote end intended by the agent.

Conclusion

Pope Saint John Paul II saw the errors of the revisionist moral theologians of his day not just as errors of the "ivory tower." Their philosophical errors lead to *moral errors*; indeed, teleologisms can be morally dangerous. Similar philosophical errors and moral dangers have cropped up again, thirty years later. For some prominent theologians and Church leaders today, the good intention of being merciful, pastoral, or loving seems to transform intrinsically evil acts, such as abortion, euthanasia, adultery, and non-marital sex, into morally acceptable or even *good* acts.[66] Grave matter baptized by good will becomes something good, rather than potentially a mortal sin. The consistent teaching of the Catholic Church, reiterated and deepened by John Paul II in *Veritatis Splendor*, however, shows this view to be unequivocally false. Theologians, Church leaders, and the lay faithful must be reminded yet again of their glorious *telos*—eternal communion with God—and the "instructions" for how to get there, including the fact that some actions are intrinsically incompatible with that end. What is at stake here is no small thing; it is eternal life.

Notes

1. See, for example, The Pontifical Academy for Life's proceedings from its 2021 seminar, published as *Theological Ethics of Life: Scripture, Tradition, and Practical Challenges* by W. Ross Hastings (Grand Rapids, MI: Zondervan, 2021), as well as a 2023 essay by Cardinal Robert McElroy in *America* magazine (24 Jan 2023).
2. John Paul II, *Veritatis Splendor* (1993), sec. 41.
3. Aquinas, *Summa Theologiae* I–II, q.91, a.2, c. Unless otherwise noted, this and subsequent citations are taken from the second and revised edition translated by the Fathers of the English Dominican Province (1920).
4. Aquinas writes: "Human reason is not, of itself, the rule of things: but the principles impressed on it by nature, are general rules and measures of all things relating to human conduct, whereof the natural reason is the rule and measure, although it is not the measure of things that are from nature." (*Summa Theologiae* I–II, q.91, a.3, ad 2). See also Russell Hittinger, "Natural Law as 'Law': Reflections on the Occasion of 'Veritatis Splendor,'" *The American Journal of Jurisprudence* 39, no. 1 (1994): 3.
5. *Veritatis Splendor*, sec. 60; see John Paul II, *Dominum et Vivificantem* (1986).
6. *Veritatis Splendor*, sec. 51.
7. *Veritatis Splendor*, sec. 51.
8. Aquinas, *Summa Theologiae* I–II, q.94, a.4, c.
9. Aquinas, *Summa Theologiae* I–II, q. 94, a.5, c.
10. See Aquinas, *Summa Theologiae* I–II, q.94, a.2, c.
11. Nevertheless, any given individual's application of the principles of the natural law can change. Aquinas notes, for instance, that "it [the natural law] is blotted out in the case of a particular action, in so far as reason is hindered from applying the general principle to a particular point of practice, on account of concupiscence or some other passion" (*Summa Theologiae* I–II, q.94, a.6, c.). For example, a person might be so overcome with rage that he takes another's life. In that case, he is blind to the principle "life is a good to be pursued," although this principle is not abolished from his heart in a general way.
12. Tianyue Wu, "Aquinas on Human Personhood and Dignity," *The Thomist* 85 (2021): 378.
13. Thomas Aquinas, I *Sentences*, d.10, q.1, a.5, c, (https://www.corpusthomisticum.org/snp1009.html#868).
14. See, for instance, Thomas Aquinas I *Sentences* d.23, q.1., a.1, c, (https://www.corpusthomisticum.org/snp1022.html).
15. See, for instance, Aquinas, *Summa Theologiae* III, q.2, a.2, ad 2.

16. Servais Pinckaers, "Aquinas on the Dignity of the Human Person" in *The Pinckaers Reader: Renewing Thomistic Moral Theology* (Washington, DC: The Catholic University of America Press, 2005), 148.
17. Aquinas, *Summa Theologiae* I–II, q. 6, a.1, c.
18. See, for example, John Paul II's essay "The Personal Structure of Self-Determination" in *Person and Community*, trans. Theresa Sandok, OSM (New York: Peter Lang, 2008), 187–195.
19. See Genesis 1:27.
20. Aquinas, *Summa Theologiae* I, q.93, a.2, c. See also Pinckaers, "Aquinas on the Dignity of the Human Person," 156, where he cites Aquinas I *Sentences* d.16, a.2.
21. Aquinas, *Summa Theologiae* I, q.93, a.1, c.
22. Pinckaers, "Aquinas on the Dignity of the Human Person."
23. Aquinas, *Summa Theologiae* I–II, q.1., a.1, c.
24. See, for instance, Ralph McInerny's helpful treatment of this matter in *Ethica Thomistica: The Moral Philosophy of Thomas Aquinas*, rev. ed. (Washington, DC: The Catholic University of America Press, 1997), 60ff.
25. *Veritatis Splendor*, sec. 71.
26. Aquinas, *Summa Theologiae* I–II, q.18, a.1, c.
27. Aquinas, *Summa Theologiae* I–II, q.18, a.4 c.
28. McInerny, *Ethica Thomistica*, 86.
29. As Steven Jensen makes clear, "'[i]ntend' simply means to 'tend into'" (p. 24). See his *Good and Evil Actions: A Journey through Saint Thomas Aquinas* (Washington, DC: The Catholic University of America Press, 2010).
30. See Romanus Cessario, OP, *Introduction to Moral Theology* (Washington, DC: The Catholic University of America Press, 2001), 176.
31. McInerny, *Ethica Thomistica*, 83.
32. See Steven Jensen's helpful account in *Good and Evil Actions*, 103–144.
33. Aquinas, *Summa Theologiae* I–II, q.7, a.1, c.
34. Aquinas, *Summa Theologiae* I–II, q.7, a.3, c.
35. Although cooking under these circumstances would make for a bad act, I am not in a position to make a judgment about the cook's moral responsibility. It may be that he is fully aware of the wildfires or is ignorant of them (vincibly or invincibly).
36. *Veritatis Splendor*, sec. 115.
37. *Veritatis Splendor*, sec. 115.
38. *Veritatis Splendor*, sec. 81.
39. *Veritatis Splendor*, sec. 78, emphasis added; see *Catechism of the Catholic Church* (Washington, DC: USCCB Publishing, 2000), sec. 1761.
40. *Veritatis Splendor*, sec. 79.
41. *Veritatis Splendor*, sec. 81.
42. Alasdair MacIntyre, "How Can We Learn What *Veritatis Splendor* Has to Teach?" *The Thomist* 58, no.2 (April 1994): 179.
43. *Veritatis Splendor*, sec. 8.

44. Matthew 19:17, emphasis added.
45. *Veritatis Splendor*, sec. 11–12.
46. John Paul II, *Reconciliatio et Poenitentia* (1984), sec. 12: "[T]here exist acts which, per se and in themselves, independently of circumstances, are always seriously wrong by reason of their object. . . . This doctrine . . . [is] based on the Decalogue."
47. *Veritatis Splendor*, sec. 13.
48. *Veritatis Splendor*, sec. 14.
49. Because of personal sin and cultural errors, not every person immediately sees these kinds of moral truths. Divine Revelation, thus, is especially helpful when morality becomes obscured.
50. *Veritatis Splendor*, sec. 80.
51. Charles Chaput, "The Splendor of Truth in 2017," *First Things* (October 2017): 8.
52. *Veritatis Splendor*, sec. 53, citing Paul VI, *Gaudium et Spes* (1965), sec. 10.
53. William May, "John Paul II, Moral Theology, and Moral Theologians," in *Veritatis Splendor and the Renewal of Moral Theology*, ed. J.A. DiNoia, OP and Romanus Cessario, OP (Princeton, NJ: Scepter Publishers, 1999), 217.
54. *Veritatis Splendor*, sec. 74–75.
55. *Veritatis Splendor*, sec. 75.
56. *Veritatis Splendor*, sec. 81.
57. *Veritatis Splendor*, sec. 80; see Thomas Aquinas, *Summa Theologiae* I–II, q.20, a.5, *sed contra*.
58. McInerny, *Ethica Thomistica*, 87.
59. For a helpful critique of consequentialism, see Josef Siefert, "The Splendor of Truth and Intrinsically Immoral Acts I: A Philosophical Defense of the Rejection of Proportionalism and Consequentialism in *Veritatis Splendor*," *Studia Philosophiae Christianae* 51 (2015). Note: This is the first of a two-article series.
60. *Veritatis Splendor*, sec. 75.
61. William Newton offers a good critique of proportionalism, especially in the context of contraception. See William Newton, "The Side Effects of the Pill: Why the Church Has So Much to Say about Contraception," *Homiletics and Pastoral Review* (21 March 2014), https://www.hprweb.com/2014/03/the-side-effects-of-the-pill-why-the-church-has-so-much-to-say-about-contraception/#fnref-9239-6.
62. *Veritatis Splendor*, sec. 65.
63. For a good treatment of the fundamental option in the context of *Veritatis splendor*, see Fr. Joseph Koterski, SJ's series of lectures entitled, "On Veritatis Splendor," *The Catholic Thing* Courses, especially Lecture 11, https://www.youtube.com/watch?v=91s7kLlKslg&list=PL6cPgDv4oM-rtr_AZh2mzjxwWnq-5UKqEc&index=11.

64. "Documentum syntheticum de moralitate nativitatum" in *The Birth Control Debate*, ed. Robert G. Hoyt (Kansas City, MO: National Catholic Reporter, 1968), 69, as cited in William May, "John Paul II, Moral Theology, and Moral Theologians," in *Veritatis Splendor and the Renewal of Moral Theology*, ed. J. A. DiNoia, OP and Romanus Cessario, OP (Princeton, NJ: Scepter Publishers, 1999), 219.

65. *Veritatis Splendor*, sec. 67.

66. See, for example, The Pontifical Academy for Life's proceedings from its 2021 seminar, published as *Theological Ethics of Life: Scripture, Tradition, and Practical Challenges* by W. Ross Hastings (Grand Rapids, MI: Zondervan, 2021), as well as a 2023 essay by Cardinal Robert McElroy in *America* magazine (24 Jan 2023).

Formation of Conscience in Veritatis Splendor

Dennis J. Billy, CSsR

John Paul II's goal in writing *Veritatis Splendor* was that of "recalling certain fundamental truths of Catholic doctrine which, in the present circumstances, risk being distorted."[1] Quoting from *Dei Verbum*, Vatican II's "Dogmatic Constitution on Divine Revelation," he asserts that *"the task of authentically interpreting the word of God, whether in its written form or in that of Tradition, has been entrusted only to those charged with the Church's living Magisterium, whose authority is exercised in the name of Jesus Christ."*[2] Quoting from the *Codex Iuris Canonici*, he further asserts that "'the Church has the right always and everywhere to proclaim moral principles, even in respect of the social order, and to make judgments about any human matter insofar as this is required by fundamental human rights or the salvation of souls.'"[3] As early as August 1, 1987, the second centenary of the death of Saint Alphonsus Liguori, the patron saint of confessors and moral theologians, John Paul II stated in his Apostolic Letter *Spiritus Domini* his intention to write an encyclical focusing on current issues in fundamental moral theology.[4] The publication of *Veritatis Splendor* was delayed until

1993, he writes, because it was fitting that the encyclical be preceded by the *Catechism of the Catholic Church*, "which contains a complete and systematic exposition of Christian moral teaching."[5] With the support of the documents of the Second Vatican Council, the *Code of Canon Law*, and the *Catechism*, he sets out in the encyclical to clarify the Church's teaching on a wide range of issues relevant to the field of fundamental moral theology. One of the most important issues he treats is the whole question of the formation of conscience, and to this topic now I turn my attention. My goal here is to give a straightforward presentation of John Paul II's thought and to show how, for him, the formation of one's conscience is an intrinsic part of the Gospel's call to conversion and conformation unto Christ.

Two Interpretive Poles

Before turning directly to John Paul II's treatment of the formation of conscience, however, it would be important to look at some of the presuppositions upon which his teaching rests. Two, in particular, stand out: (1) that the moral law comes from God and we share in it by means of "*theonomy*" or a "*participated theonomy*"[6] and (2) our minds have been darkened and our wills, weakened as a consequence of Original Sin, and hence, our capacity to know the moral truth has been inhibited.[7] A look at each of these presuppositions will help us to better appreciate John Paul II's magisterial teaching on conscience formation.

A Theonomous Ethic

To say that the moral law consists of a "theonomy" or a "participated theonomy" means that it comes from God but has, at the same time, been implanted deep within the human heart. This approach seeks to offset two false notions of the moral law: (1) that it consists solely in our use of reason and is, therefore, an autonomous ethic and (2) that it is imposed from without with no relation to human reason at all and is, therefore, a heteronomous ethic. Each of these understandings of the moral law has liabilities and, as John Paul II points out, does not resonate with authentic Catholic teaching.

An autonomous ethic, which confines the moral law to human reason alone and with no reference to God, places us at the center of the moral universe and gives us the right to determine what is good and what is evil. Such an approach leads to subjectivism and moral relativism (what John Paul II's successor, Benedict XVI, then Cardinal Joseph Ratzinger, called the "dictatorship of relativism"[8]) and is reminiscent of the sin of Adam and Eve, who, by eating the forbidden fruit of the tree of the knowledge of good and evil, sought to seize for themselves what God alone could determine.[9] While it is true that "God in the beginning created human beings and made them subject to their own free choice" (Sir 15:14), man's rightful autonomy is not absolute but limited. "*The moral law,*" John Paul II states, "*has its origin in God and always finds its source in him.*"[10] Quoting from an address to a group of bishops from the United States on their *ad limina* visit, he states that "the autonomy of reason cannot mean that reason itself creates values and moral norms."[11] These come from God alone and no one else.

A heteronomous ethic, by way of contrast, imposes the moral law from without and makes man "subject to the will of something all-powerful, absolute, extraneous to man and intolerant of his freedom."[12] John Paul II goes on to say: "If in fact a heteronomy of morality were to mean a denial of man's self-determination or the imposition of norms unrelated to his good, this would be in contradiction to the Revelation of the Covenant and of the redemptive Incarnation."[13] A heteronomous ethic makes us slaves to a more powerful person who imposes his will on us and forces us to follow his commands. Such a person could be an all-powerful but frivolous and loveless God who, as William of Ockham, the fourteenth-century Franciscan theologian, imagined, could invert the relationship between good and evil in an instant simply by willing it. An entity such as a dictatorial state would be another example of how an extraneous set of values and norms could be imposed from without and not consider the citizens' right to self-determination.[14]

By stating that the moral law comes from God but is implanted in our heart, a theonomous ethic steers clear of the dangers of false autonomy and reckless heteronomy. It affirms the existence of human nature and a law placed in the human heart that is nothing but a natural participation or sharing in the Eternal Law itself. It avoids the dangers of subjectivism and moral relativism by insisting on the existence of objective moral truth. It affirms, moreover, that obedience to the moral law is an act of love rather blind obedience to a person or entity who wields the power to punish and even kill.

A Fallen World

John Paul II opens his encyclical with one of the foundational anthropological truths of the Catholic faith: "The splendor of truth shines forth in all the works of the Creator and, in a special way, in man, created in the image and likeness of God (cf. *Gen* 1:26)."[15] Because we reflect God's image and likeness, we are capable of entering into a personal relationship with

Him and share in the intimacy of His divine love. We are, in other words, "capable of God" (*capax Dei*) and able to share in His divine nature. We are made holy through "obedience to the truth (1 *Pet* 22)"[16] and find true freedom "in the Truth."[17]

John Paul II goes on to say that despite our noble stature, "this obedience is not always easy."[18] The reason why it is not always easy is our human sinfulness:

> As a result of that mysterious original sin, committed at the prompting of Satan, the one who is "a liar and the father of lies" (*Jn* 8:44), man is constantly tempted to turn his gaze away from the living and true God in order to direct it towards idols (cf. 1Thes 1:9), exchanging "the truth about God for a lie" (Rom 1:25).[19]

As a result of Original Sin, our noble nature has been wounded: "Man's capacity to know the truth is also darkened, and his will to submit to it is weakened. Thus, giving himself over to relativism and skepticism (cf. *Jn* 18:38), he goes off in search of an illusory freedom apart from truth itself."[20]

As a result of Original Sin, our nature was wounded but not totally corrupted. As John Paul II states, "No darkness of error or of sin can totally take away from man the light of God the Creator. In the depths of his heart there always remains a yearning for absolute truth and a thirst to attain full knowledge of it."[21] What is more, there is "an imperishable spark," a spark of the soul (*scintilla animae*) that urges him always to do good and avoid evil. This spark of the soul is the deepest level of conscience and is what Thomas Aquinas calls "synderesis," a habit of the practical intellect that holds the primary principles of the natural law.[22] Later in the encyclical, John Paul II refers directly to the command not to eat the fruit from the tree of the knowledge of good and evil given by God to our first parents and connects it to our desire for unlimited freedom:

> Revelation teaches that *the power to decide what is good and what is evil does not belong to man, but to God alone.* The man is certainly free, inasmuch as he can understand and accept God's commands. And he possesses an extremely far-reaching freedom since he can eat "of every tree of the garden." But his freedom is not unlimited: it must halt before the "tree of the knowledge of good and evil;" for it is called to accept the moral law given by God.[23]

As a result of the Fall, we no longer see clearly the moral truths set forth by God that so enlightened our minds at the dawn of creation. Because of the Fall, the flame of our moral sense has been dimmed, although not completely extinguished. Because of the Fall, there was a need for God to reveal His Word to the people of Israel, through Abraham and his descendants, through Moses and the prophets, and ultimately, in the person of Jesus Christ, who was the Son of God and the Word-Made-Flesh. Because of the Fall, God sent His only begotten Son to redeem humanity, indeed, all of creation, by dying on the Cross for us, rising from the dead, ascending into heaven, giving us His Spirit to help us to see the moral law more clearly, and empowering us to keep it. In doing so, God brings good out of evil. At the Easter Vigil, the priest or deacon sings the *Exsultet* and refers to the sin of Adam and Eve as "O happy fault, that earned so great, so glorious a Redeemer!"[24] The Fall, we might say, makes possible the redemption of humanity and all creation. Evil has no power over the Lord of the Universe. Satan, the father of lies, has been defeated by Jesus, who is "the way and the truth and the life" (Jn 14:6).

What Is Conscience?

If the notion of "theonomy" or "participated theonomy" and the Catholic doctrine of the Fall are two interpretive poles around which the topic of the formation of conscience rotates, it is equally important that, before discussing the formation of conscience, we have a clear understanding of just what John Paul II means by the term "conscience." Although he is quick to point out that "the Church's Magisterium does not intend to impose upon the faithful any particular theological system, still less a philosophical one,"[25] it is clear when reading *Veritatis Splendor* that Pope Saint John Paul II relies heavily on the thought of Thomas Aquinas. Although he quotes many of the Fathers and Doctors of the Church throughout the encyclical, the thought of the Angelic Doctor is by far the most prevalent and upon which John Paul II relies most heavily.

When discussing "conscience," John Paul II quotes a pivotal text from *Gaudium et Spes* ("The Pastoral Constitution on the Church in the Modern World"):

> In the depths of his conscience man detects a law which he does not impose on himself, but which holds him to obedience. Always summoning him to love good and avoid evil, the voice of conscience can, when necessary, speak to his heart more specifically: "do this, shun that." For man has in his heart a law written by God. To obey it is the very dignity of man; according to it he will be judged (cf. *Rom* 2:14-16).[26]

The law written in our hearts is not imposed blindly from without (as in the case of heteronomy), nor have we written it by ourselves (as in the case of autonomy). It comes from God (as in the case of theonomy).

Conscience for John Paul II is a capacity, a process, and a judgment. Let us examine these in reverse order. Following Aquinas, John Paul II calls conscience "a practical judgment, a judgment which makes known what man must do or not do, or which assesses an act already performed by him."[27] The former, a judgment about an action yet to be performed, is often referred to as "legislative conscience," while the latter, a judgment about an action already performed, is often referred to as "judicial conscience."

In addition to being a practical judgment, conscience is also a process of deliberation or, to be more precise, an interior dialogue: "The importance of this interior *dialogue of man with himself* can never be adequately appreciated. But it is also a *dialogue of man with God*, the author of the law. The primordial image and final end of man."[28] Notice that this dialogue is not merely with oneself but with oneself and God. This dialogue has to do with applying the objective moral truth to concrete situations. This objective moral truth comes from God and is not something that we compose and, therefore, is not open to subjective moral relativism.

Finally, conscience is also a capacity, what Aquinas calls "synderesis," a habit of the practical intellect containing the primary principle of the natural law.[29] This "imperishable spark (*scintilla animae*) shines in the heart of every man."[30] It can be dimmed or tarnished due to sin and, thus, impede man's ability to discern moral truth, but it can never be fully extinguished. As a result, conscience "thus formulates *moral obligation* in the light of the natural law; it is the obligation to do what the individual, through the workings of his conscience, *knows* to be a good he is called to do *here and now*."[31]

The practical judgment of conscience flows from our capacity to know the principles of the natural law and the dialogue we have with God concerning how these principles should be applied in particular instances: "Consequently *in the practical judgment of conscience*, which imposes on the person the obligation to perform a given act, *the link between freedom and truth is made manifest.*"[32] Conscience, in other words, brings us face-to-face with objective moral truth and bids us to act responsibly in accordance with that truth in the concrete circumstances of daily life. It is not, as some modern thinkers assert, a function of our subjective autonomy with no reference whatsoever to the objective moral order.

The Formation of Conscience

Now that we know what conscience is, as presented in *Veritatis Splendor*, we are in a position to look at what John Paul II says about the formation of conscience. To begin with, it bears noting that the very use of the word "formation" indicates that the judgment of conscience is something that requires a process of development, a search, a movement from uncertainty to clarity about how one should apply the natural law in specific circumstances. The *formation* of conscience, in other words, has to do with applying the various precepts of natural law to particular cases that an individual has encountered in the past, present, or future. That law, as we have seen, comes from God but has been implanted in the minds and hearts of every human being. The basic precepts of this law include doing good and avoiding evil, self-preservation, procreation and the education of offspring, and life in society and the search for truth and justice. The Decalogue or Ten Commandments, which were revealed by God, are also constituent elements of this natural law and provide added certainty to human minds and hearts whose capacity for knowing the truth by the light of human reason and implementing it have been weakened as a result of the consequences of Original Sin and that may have been further hindered by a life of personal sin and steeped in a society that has been hampered by sinful social structures.

Because of our weakened and wounded condition, the judgment of conscience can either be correct or erroneous. It is correct when the application of natural law, strengthened by the certitude of Divine Revelation, applies natural law to specific cases in a way that resonates with the truth. As a dialogue with God, this judgment meets specific criteria such as those required for the principle of double effect: (1) the object of the action is good in and of itself (or, at least, neutral), (2) the intention of the action is good, (3) the end does not justify the means, and (4) there is a proportional reason for producing an evil side effect. The judgment of conscience is erroneous when it does not live up to the standards of objective morality and can be either *culpably erroneous* or due to *invincible ignorance*.[33] The former occurs "when man shows little concern for seeking what is true and good, and conscience becomes almost blind from being accustomed to sin."[34] The latter occurs because, conscience not being an infallible judge, there enters "an ignorance of which the subject is not aware and which he is unable to overcome himself."[35] John Paul II goes on to say: "The Council reminds us that in cases where such invincible ignorance is not culpable, conscience does not lose its dignity, because even when it directs us to act in a way not in conformity with the objective moral order, it continues to speak in the name of that truth about the good which the subject is called to seek sincerely."[36] John Paul II makes it clear, however, that such actions of an erroneous conscience due to invincible ignorance cannot in any way be considered salvific or meritorious. Following the teaching of Aquinas, he says "it is never acceptable to confuse a 'subjective' error about a moral good with the 'objective' truth."[37] This coincides with the teaching of Pseudo-Dionysius, which was also held by Aquinas, that "good results from an entire cause, whereas evil arises from each single defect."[38] In other words, for an action to be considered meritorious, it must be good in all respects. A single defect renders it lacking in such worth.

In most circumstances, the formation of conscience should present little difficulty whatsoever, since our wounded nature (and, therefore, conscience) has the added help of Divine Revelation (the Ten Commandments, Jesus's Sermon on the Mount) and the teaching of the Church Magisterium.[39] It would be an expression of pride, reflective of the sin of our first parents, to neglect these additional helps in favor of our own subjective and autonomous rendering of the moral truth in such-and-such particular situation. To do so would be to place ourselves at the center of the moral universe and, in effect, make the same mistake made by Adam and Eve: to appropriate for ourselves a right that belongs only to God—determining what is good and what is evil.[40] In presuming to take this power to ourselves, we seek to be like God and would, thus, rupture the Creator-creature relationship that marks our very existence. We seek, in other words, an absolute autonomy rather than the limited autonomy given to us by God as a result of our creaturely status.

Examining formation of conscience from a wider perspective, John Paul II views it as "the object of a continuous conversion to what is true and to what is good."⁴¹ In this respect, he refers to Saint Paul's exhortation to the Romans "not to be conformed to the mentality of the world, but to be transformed by the renewal of our mind (cf. *Rom* 12:2)."⁴² For John Paul II, the formation of conscience is all about "the 'heart' converted to the Lord and to the love of what is good which is really the source of *true* judgments of conscience."⁴³ Later in his encyclical, he will identify this fundamental conversion of heart as the true fundamental option in a person's life, distinguishing it from false notions of it that were promoted by some twentieth-century theologians who sought to separate one's transcendental (vertical) relationship with the Divine from one's categorical (horizontal) actions in the world, thus largely doing away with objective morality and blurring (and even doing away with) the distinction between moral and venial sin.⁴⁴

As important as the knowledge of God's law is, John Paul II is quick to point out that "knowledge of God's law in general is certainly necessary, but it is not sufficient."⁴⁵ The moral life, in his mind, consists in much more than merely making practical judgments that apply the natural law to specific situations. "What is essential," he claims, "is a sort of '*connaturality*' *between man and the true good.*"⁴⁶ Since the true good is God Himself, this connaturality involves being rooted in and growing in a life of virtue, which includes "prudence, and the other cardinal virtues, and even before these the theological virtues of faith, hope, and charity."⁴⁷

When seen in this light, the formation of conscience is but one aspect of the formation of the human person, whose destiny and final end is the beatific vision, an intimate participation in the divine life that manifests itself in an intimate friendship with the Triune God. In the end, it all has to do with Jesus's words to the rich young man in the opening chapter of *Veritatis Splendor*: "Follow me."

> As he calls the young man to follow him along the way of perfection, Jesus asks him to be perfect in the command of love, in "his" commandment: to become part of the unfolding of his complete giving, to imitate and rekindle the very love of the "Good" Teacher, the one who loved "to the end." This is what Jesus asks of everyone who wishes to follow him.[48]

The moral life ultimately means "*becoming conformed to him* [Christ]."[49] This may seem impossible to achieve by human effort alone, but "all things are possible with God" (Mt 19:26),[50] and Jesus has given us His Spirit who, through Baptism, "radically configures the faithful to Christ in the Paschal Mystery of death and resurrection."[51] What is more, the Sacrament of the Eucharist furthers our assimilation to Christ who is

> the source of eternal life (cf. *Jn* 6:51–58), the source and power of the complete gift of self, which Jesus—according to the testimony handed on by Paul—commands us to commemorate in liturgy and in life: "As often as you eat this bread and drink the cup, you proclaim the Lord's death and resurrection until he comes" (1 *Cor* 11:26).[52]

The moral life, in other words, culminates in life in the Spirit, who orients our whole lives toward Christ and who bestows upon us His myriad gifts and fruits, all of which enable us to respond spontaneously to His promptings and conform ourselves to Christ in a way we could never do by ourselves alone.

Some Observations

After this presentation of the presuppositions John Paul II makes regarding his understanding of formation of conscience, a treatment of conscience itself, and the process of forming one's conscience, we are now in a position to make some remarks concerning its effect on other matters treated in *Veritatis Splendor*. These observations are not meant to be exhaustive but merely point to the importance the formation of conscience plays in John Paul II's overall conception of fundamental moral theology.

Conscience formation is a part of a larger process of the formation of the human person to be conformed unto Christ. Jesus's call to discipleship and exhortation to follow Him extends to every human being. When seen in this light, the moral life is rooted in a personal relationship with Christ and His commandment to love God with our whole heart, mind, and soul, and to love our neighbor as ourselves. The moral life, in other words, is rooted in the objective reality of Christ, the Word-Made-Flesh and Eternal Word of the Father. This reality exists outside of our subjective reality and is written in our hearts. We are "capable of God" (*capax Dei*) and, therefore, able, with the assistance of God's grace, to enter into an intimate relationship with the Divine.[53] Jesus no longer calls us servants, but friends. Leading the moral life is an expression of our love for Christ and our desire to enter into such a relationship.

As presented in Veritatis Splendor, *the formation of conscience rests on the pillars of theonomy and the Catholic doctrine of the Fall.* The former is the way John Paul II steers clear of the exaggerated extremes of an autonomous and heteronomous ethic, while the latter emphasizes our wounded nature and weakened conscience and the need for Divine Revelation to assist us in coming to a clear understanding of the moral law. This law is a participation in the Eternal Law, Who is none other than the Word of God, the *Logos* of the Father. For this reason, the moral law comes from God alone and cannot be reduced to either a subjective relativistic autonomy or a purely imposed authority without anything about it resonating from within. When seen in this light, conscience is the mediator between truth and freedom. It is not freedom *from the truth* but freedom *in the truth*.[54]

The above distinction is reminiscent of Servais Pinckaers's discussion of the difference between the "freedom of indifference" and the "freedom for excellence."[55] While the former posits a human anthropology rooted solely in an autonomous will that seeks to be radically free from anything imposed on it either from without or from within, the latter understands freedom in terms of the power to do the Good. The example of someone learning how to play the violin is an apt metaphor for what Pinckaers means by the "freedom for excellence." To learn how to play the instrument, a beginner must spend hours learning both how to read music and then how to play it. After months of practicing, he is able to play increasingly complex pieces of music, while still reading off the music sheets. In time, he is able to free himself from the written music and is able to play the instrument spontaneously. After still more time, he can improvise and compose beautiful works all by himself. As we shall see in the next observation, living the moral life involves a similar process.

Placed in the context of continuous conversion and the threefold way of purgation, illumination, and union, the formation of conscience corresponds to the early, purgative stage of the journey, which deals with the cleansing of one's heart and the following of the Commandments. Although each stage is subsumed into the one following it, the normal way of understanding this process of continual conversion is that the way of purgation corresponds to the Commandments, while that of illumination consists in following a life of virtue, and the way of union, being open to the gifts of the Spirit. When seen in this light, the formation of conscience is important at every stage of the spiritual journey yet becomes easier as we draw closer to Christ and are more open to the movements of the Spirit in our lives.

Thomas Aquinas considers law an analogous concept. In his treatise on law, he speaks about the different kinds of law, all of which bear certain similarities and differences.[56] There is an eternal law (a. 1), a natural law (a. 2), a human law (a. 3), a divine law (aa. 4–5), and a law of sin (a. 6). Most importantly, there is the evangelical law, which is primarily the grace of the Holy Spirit and secondarily, the written law of the Gospel.[57] When speaking of the moral life, it is important to note that, because of our wounded condition, we cannot fulfill the requirements of even the natural law without the assistance of the grace of the Holy Spirit. As we move along the way of holiness, we become more open to this grace which, in turn, leads us more deeply into a life of virtue and openness to the myriad gifts, fruits, and promptings of the Holy Spirit. John Paul II's thinking on the formation of conscience presupposes these distinctions and recognizes that the moral life is, first and foremost, life in the Spirit that follows the New Law that comes to a person through faith in Christ.[58]

The structural placement of John Paul II's treatment of the formation of conscience in chapter two, "Do Not Be Conformed to This World (Rom 12:2)," tells us something about the role it plays in dealing with "certain tendencies in present-day moral theology."[59] After an Introduction that lays the groundwork for what lies ahead, the chapter is divided into four major sections: (1) "Freedom and Law," (2) "Conscience and Truth," (3) "Fundamental Choice and Specific Kinds of Behavior," and (4) "The Moral Act." In the first section, John Paul II argues in favor of theonomy (as opposed to autonomy or heteronomy),[60] insists human freedom is not absolute but limited in nature and must answer to this objective moral order,[61] asserts the body/soul unity of the human person,[62] recognizes an objective moral law and the universality of the natural law,[63] claims the universal and exceptionless binding nature of the negative precepts of the Decalogue,[64] and recognizes the transcendent nature of man that enables him to rise above the particular culture to which he belongs.[65] The second section, "Conscience and Truth," builds on these claims in making conscience the mediator between freedom and law, thus enabling John Paul II to confront dissenting opinions from the authoritative teaching of the Living Magisterium.

John Paul II writes the encyclical to set forth clearly the principles of Catholic fundamental moral theology as set forth in Sacred Scripture and the living Apostolic Tradition.[66] In doing so, he also seeks "to shed light on the presuppositions and consequences of the dissent which that teaching has met."[67] His teaching on the formation of conscience is one of the primary ways in which he upholds the existence of an objective moral order and responds to the contemporary movement toward subjective relativism as manifest and the interpretation of the fundamental option that separates a person's relationship to the transcendental (vertical) order and the categorical (horizontal) order, thus blurring the distinction between mortal sin and venial sin, as well as their validity, and drawing a wedge between the ethical order and the order of salvation.[68] It is also a primary means by which he responds to the erroneous doctrines of proportionalism and consequentialism. If theonomy and the Catholic doctrine of the Fall provide the theological presuppositions for the formation of conscience, the latter offers the practical means by which these presuppositions enter the moral order.

The encyclical deals with the errors of proportionalism and consequentialism by reaffirming the existence of an objective moral order and the added principle that the end does not justify the means,[69] *two elements of the principle of double effect that these theories denied.* Although John Paul II does not directly deal with the principle of double effect, he reinstates two of its key elements and, thus, undermines the position of these dissenting teachings by pointing out that they ultimately lead to subjective relativism and a morality that fuses the object of the act with its intention, rather than as seeing them separately as "what was done" (object) and "why" it was done (intention).[70] John Paul II is clear that, while the morality of a human act depends on the intention, circumstances, and the object,[71] it is the latter, defined as "the proximate end of a deliberate decision which determines the act of willing on the part of the acting person,"[72] that specifies the act and determines whether or not an action can be intrinsically evil.[73] What is more, John Paul II takes on one of the fundamental claims of these theories. Contrary to their position, he states, "Everyone recognizes the difficulty, or rather the impossibility, of evaluating all the good and evil consequences and effects—defined as pre-moral—of one's acts: an exhaustive rational calculation is not possible."[74]

In dealing with a culpable erroneous conscience and non-culpable invincible ignorance, John Paul II chooses not to treat certain delicate areas. Although he recognizes that conscience is the *"proximate norm of personal morality"*[75] and says that our conscience is *culpably erroneous* when we show "little concern for seeking what is true and good, and conscience gradually becomes almost blind from being accustomed to sin,"[76] he does not treat a situation in which we sincerely struggle to seek what is true and good but still cannot accept the teaching of the Church. Following Aquinas, John Paul II states that we are bound to follow our conscience in such circumstances but that the action cannot be considered meritorious.[77] However, he does not treat the alternative, tutiorist view put forth by Saint Bonaventure that in such a situation, we are bound to change our conscience in conformity with the teaching of the Church, or the equiprobable position of Saint Alphonsus de Liguori that, precisely because conscience is the proximate personal norm of morality, those of us with an invincibly ignorant conscience are bound to follow our conscience and perform an action that may, in the end, even prove to be meritorious.[78]

In chapter three, "Lest the Cross of Christ Be Emptied of Its Power," John Paul II says that Christian martyrdom is "an affirmation of the inviolability of the moral order," because it *"rejects as false and illusory whatever 'human meaning' one might claim to attribute, even in 'exceptional' conditions, to an act morally evil in itself,"* [79] and is, therefore, *"an outstanding sign of the holiness of the Church."*[80] The same holds true for the formation of conscience which, earlier in the encyclical, he describes as "a witness of his [man's] faithfulness or unfaithfulness with regard to the law, of his essential moral rectitude or iniquity."[81] Here, John Paul II is implicitly referring to the distinction between "red" and "white" martyrdom, whereby the former gives witness to Christ through the spilling of blood, while the latter gives witness to Him not through the spilling of blood but by taking up one's cross and following Him. Jesus and Mary are examples, respectively, par excellence of red and white martyrdom. John Paul II uses this example to demonstrate that living the moral life and forming one's conscience accordingly is a clear example of giving witness to Christ in a world seemingly overcome by the force of evil and the darkness of sin.

Conclusion

John Paul II's treatment of the formation of conscience in *Veritatis Splendor* appears at a critical point in the encyclical. Placed in the second chapter where he seeks to shed light on the presuppositions and consequences of many of the erroneous teachings of dissent regarding fundamental areas of Church teaching, it reinforces traditional Catholic teaching and uses conscience formation as a tool to point out the weaknesses in certain positions of Catholic moral theologians in the post-Vatican II era. Numbered among these opinions are the notion of fundamental option, the disconnect between the order of salvation (the transcendental) and the moral order (the categorical), the theories of proportionalism and consequentialism, the denial of the existence of intrinsically evil acts, and the blurring (or outright discarding) of the distinction between mortal and venial sin. The greatest strength of John Paul II's teaching is that it reaffirms the existence of an objective moral order that, revealed by God and imprinted in every man's heart, avoids the dangers of moral relativism, whereby man makes himself (not God) the center of the moral universe.

If Pope Saint Paul VI's 1968 post-Vatican II encyclical *Humanae Vitae*[82] ushered in a time when Catholic moral theologians, in addition to raising doubts about the unity of the procreative and unitive meaning of the conjugal act, also began to seriously question such issues as the authority of the Magisterium to teach in moral matters (and especially in areas regarding natural law) and the right to dissent from non-infallible, reformable magisterial teachings, then John Paul II's 1993 encyclical, *Veritatis Splendor*, brought clarity to the field of fundamental moral theology by reaffirming the Church's traditional teaching and presenting it in a way that could answer the objections of dissenting theologians and help the faithful understand more deeply the teachings of the Church in the areas under question. His teaching on theonomy, the existence of an objective moral order, and the formation of a correct conscience contributed greatly to bringing order into this state of confusion. When seen in this light, *Humanae Vitae* and *Veritatis Splendor* can be looked upon as sturdy and well-founded magisterial bookends that help us understand the turmoil in the field of fundamental moral theology during the twenty-five-year period between 1968 and 1993. That is not to say that all questions have been resolved or that dissent did not continue in certain theological circles. However, with his 1993 encyclical, John Paul II spoke with the authority of the living Magisterium on topics that had never before been raised and brought into question by moral theologians. We can say that the questions raised during this time caused the Magisterium to reflect more deeply on certain areas of its moral teaching by providing sound philosophical and theological foundations upon which this teaching was based.

In the final analysis, John Paul II's teaching on the formation of conscience in *Veritatis Splendor* is a practical tool that provides the faithful with clear directions on how to form a correct conscience in line with the teachings of the Church. Through the use of theonomy and the Catholic doctrine of the Fall, it affirms the existence of an objective moral order and provides clear guidelines for mediating the relationship between truth and freedom. It recognizes that human freedom is not absolute and understands that because of humanity's wounded and weakened condition, conscience itself is subject to error. Be that as it may, John Paul II affirms that it is never permissible "to confuse a 'subjective' error about the moral good with the 'objective' truth."[83]

NOTES

1. John Paul II, *Veritatis Splendor* (1993), sec. 4.
2. *Veritatis Splendor*, sec. 27.
3. *Veritatis Splendor*, referencing *Canon Law*, Canon 747, 2.
4. *Veritatis Splendor*, sec. 5.
5. *Veritatis Splendor*, sec. 5.
6. *Veritatis Splendor*, sec. 41.
7. *Veritatis Splendor*, sec. 1.
8. "Homily of His Eminence Cardinal Joseph Ratzinger Dean of the College of Cardinals," (Vatican Basilica, April 18, 2005), https://www.vatican.va/gpII/documents/homily-pro-eligendo-pontifice_20050418_en.html.
9. *Veritatis Splendor*, sec. 35.
10. *Veritatis Splendor*, sec. 40.
11. *Veritatis Splendor*, sec. 40.
12. *Veritatis Splendor*, sec. 41.
13. *Veritatis Splendor*, sec. 41.
14. *Veritatis Splendor*, sec. 41. See also Servais Pinckaers, *The Sources of Christian Ethics*, trans. Mary Thomas Noble (Washington, DC: The Catholic University of America Press, 1995), 240–53.
15. *Veritatis Splendor*, opening paragraph.
16. *Veritatis Splendor*, sec. 1.
17. *Veritatis Splendor*, sec. 64.
18. *Veritatis Splendor*, sec. 1.
19. *Veritatis Splendor*, sec. 1.
20. *Veritatis Splendor*, sec. 1.
21. *Veritatis Splendor*, sec. 1.
22. Thomas Aquinas, *Summa Theologiae*, I, q. 79, a. 12, resp.
23. *Veritatis Splendor*, sec. 35.
24. *The Roman Missal*, Approved by the United States Conference of Bishops and Confirmed by the Apostolic See (Italy: Magnificat-Desclée, 2011), 342.
25. *Veritatis Splendor*, sec. 29.
26. *Veritatis Splendor*, sec. 54.; Second Vatican Council, *Gaudium et Spes* (1965), sec.16.
27. *Veritatis Splendor*, sec. 59; Aquinas, *Summa Theologiae*, I, q. 79, a. 13, resp.
28. *Veritatis Splendor*, sec. 58.
29. Aquinas, *Summa Theologiae*, I, q. 79, a.12, resp.
30. *Veritatis Splendor*, sec. 59.
31. *Veritatis Splendor*, sec. 59.
32. *Veritatis Splendor*, sec. 60.
33. *Veritatis Splendor*, sec. 62–63.

34. *Veritatis Splendor*, sec. 63.
35. *Veritatis Splendor*, sec. 62.
36. *Veritatis Splendor*, sec. 62.
37. *Veritatis Splendor*, sec. 63. See also Thomas Aquinas *De Veritate*, q. 17, a. 4.
38. Pseudo-Dionysius the Areopagite, *The Divine Names*, 4.30; Aquinas, *Summa Theologiae*, II–II, q. 79, a. 3, ad 4.
39. *Veritatis Splendor*, sec. 27, 64.
40. See Genesis 3: 4–5.
41. *Veritatis Splendor*, sec. 64.
42. *Veritatis Splendor*, sec. 64.
43. *Veritatis Splendor*, sec. 64.
44. *Veritatis Splendor*, sec. 66–69.
45. *Veritatis Splendor*, sec. 64.
46. *Veritatis Splendor*, sec. 64.
47. *Veritatis Splendor*, sec. 64.
48. *Veritatis Splendor*, sec. 20.
49. *Veritatis Splendor*, sec. 21.
50. *Veritatis Splendor*, sec. 22.
51. *Veritatis Splendor*, sec. 21.
52. *Veritatis Splendor*, sec. 21.
53. See Aquinas, *Summa Theologiae*, I–II, q. 113, a, 10, resp. See also St. Augustine, *De Trinitate*. 14.8.
54. *Veritatis Splendor*, sec. 64.
55. Pinckaers, *The Sources of Christian Ethics*, 375.
56. Aquinas, *Summa Theologiae*, I–II, q. 91.
57. Aquinas, *Summa Theologiae*, I–II, q. 106, a. 3, resp.
58. *Veritatis Splendor*, sec. 21, 23–24.
59. *Veritatis Splendor*, chap. 2, title, emphasis added.
60. *Veritatis Splendor*, sec. 41.
61. *Veritatis Splendor*, sec. 41.
62. *Veritatis Splendor*, sec. 48.
63. *Veritatis Splendor*, sec. 51.
64. *Veritatis Splendor*, sec. 52.
65. *Veritatis Splendor*, sec. 53.
66. *Veritatis Splendor*, sec. 5.
67. *Veritatis Splendor*, sec. 5.
68. *Veritatis Splendor*, sec. 37.
69. *Veritatis Splendor*, sec. 77–79.
70. *Veritatis Splendor*, sec. 74.
71. *Veritatis Splendor*, sec. 74.
72. *Veritatis Splendor*, sec. 78.
73. *Veritatis Splendor*, sec. 78.
74. *Veritatis Splendor*, sec. 77.

75. *Veritatis Splendor*, sec. 60.
76. *Veritatis Splendor*, sec. 62.
77. *Veritatis Splendor*, sec. 63.
78. See Dennis J. Billy, "The Authority of Conscience in Bonaventure and Aquinas," *Studia Moralia* 31(1993): 237–63. See also Alphonsus de Liguori, *Theologia Moralis*, Bk. 1, chap.1, aa. 5–6.
79. *Veritatis Splendor*, sec. 92, emphasis added.
80. *Veritatis Splendor*, sec. 93.
81. *Veritatis Splendor*, sec. 57.
82. Paul VI, *Humanae Vitae* (1968).
83. *Veritatis Splendor*, sec. 63.

Veritatis Splendor and Pastoral Accompaniment: Diakonia Veritatis and the Art of Speaking the Truth in Love

Thomas Berg

Reference to "accompaniment" appears only in a few places in *Veritatis Splendor*. Of particular importance are these two passages:

> The Church's Pastors, in communion with the Successor of Peter, are close to the faithful in this effort [of announcing Christ to the world]; they guide and *accompany them by their authoritative teaching*, finding ever new ways of speaking with love and mercy not only to believers but to all people of good will.[1]

> The unacceptability of "teleological", "consequentialist" and "proportionalist" ethical theories, which deny the existence of negative moral norms regarding specific kinds of behavior, norms which are valid without exception, is confirmed in a particularly eloquent way by *Christian martyrdom, which has always accompanied and continues to accompany the life of the Church* even today.[2]

I develop the following reflections within the framework of these references to accompaniment: the Church accompanying the faithful through the continual proclamation of true moral teaching, particularly through the Magisterium, and the martyrs accompanying the faithful as the "great cloud of witnesses" (Heb 12:1), giving testimony—with their blood—to unchanging moral truths.

I will also develop these reflections in tension with contemporary revisionist moral theology that continues the broad project of proportionalist moral theologians, particularly in their insistence on the centrality of a problematic understanding of conscience as the foundation of the moral life.[3] What is at stake here goes much deeper than questions of how to deal pastorally with the divorced and remarried, or whether the Church can or cannot declare some marriage bonds dissolved; it involves our understanding of underlying anthropological presuppositions including, but not limited to, our concepts of conscience, freedom, the moral qualification of human actions, what it means to exist as sexed beings, and the nature of moral progress and human flourishing.

The contention among many revisionist moral theologians and bishops is that even the least insistence on any of these truths or on the applicability of any relevant moral norm constitutes reversion to an intolerable ethic of rule-following, an ethic putatively in tension with the "lived reality" of real individuals, and incompatible with a sound pastoral sensitivity and personalistic approach to morality. Specifically, revisionist moral theology appears to presuppose that there is a tension, not to say an incompatibility, between pastoral care (accompaniment), on the one hand, and doctrine (moral truths as perennially taught by the Church), on the other. In what follows, I hope, at least, to offer a brief sketch of why such thinking is simply out of touch with the project of genuinely Christic pastoral accompaniment.

No Conflict between "Pastoral Care" (Accompaniment) and "Doctrine" (Moral Truth)

The supposed tension between pastoral accompaniment and the presentation of moral truths—the presentation and explication of moral norms—is not only unsound; it has no basis in Sacred Scripture nor in the Church's lived experience of genuine *agape*-love for our brothers and sisters as witnessed to by the lives of the saints.

Cardinal Raymond Burke, in a recent essay, has testified to the reality of a rhetoric and train of thought—broadly speaking, to be found among some theologians and bishops—that posits this tension between doctrine and pastoral care. He observes:

> Pastoral care is now regularly contrasted with concern for the doctrine, which must be its foundation. The concern for doctrine and discipline is characterized as pharisaical, as wishing to respond coldly or even violently to the faithful who find themselves in an irregular situation morally and canonically. In this errant view, mercy is opposed to justice, listening is opposed to teaching, and discernment is opposed to judgment.[4]

To be sure, Pope Francis himself has often given the lie to such a conception of things. He did so as recently as last year, returning from World Youth Day in Lisbon. In his in-flight comments, he responded to a reporter's assertion that, in fact, not all people appear to be "welcome" in the Church because not all are allowed to participate in the sacraments. The Pope responded:

> The Church is open for everyone. Then there is legislation that regulates life inside the Church. Someone inside follows the legislation. What you say is a simplification: "They cannot participate in the sacraments." This does not mean that the Church is closed. Everyone meets God on their own way inside the Church, and the Church is Mother and guides everyone on their own path.... Everyone, everyone in prayer, in inner dialogue, in pastoral dialogue, looks for the way forward.[5]

The use of the term "legislation" was, perhaps, an attempt to speak in terminology that the reporter could understand, but obviously it was not the best term. "Legislation" is essentially reducible to "policy" that can be changed by the fiat of the legislators. It does not get at the firm metaphysical ground and rational basis for moral norms, many of which are exceptionless, universal, and unchanging. Word choice aside, his point is most valid. While acknowledging that, yes, the Church is welcoming, he, nonetheless, upholds the reality of moral normativity. And when the Holy Father has often condemned abortion (in extremely strong language) or when he has condemned the cultural imposition of gender ideology as "ideological colonization," he certainly is working with a concept of moral norms and of behaviors that are always and, in every case, intrinsically disordered.

But as we will see in a final point, the question is: today, how do we speak the truth in love? How do we communicate the truth effectively in a manner that it can be accepted?

Contemporary Revisionism, Exceptionless Moral Norms, and a Revolutionary Understanding of Conscience

What revisionist moral theologians offer is an approach seemingly heavy on pastoral sensitivity. Yet, by opting to relax any insistence on moral normativity, they obscure the very understanding of moral norms and their place in the moral life. In a word, revisionism opens an enormous space between norms and the concrete situations of the individual. Adopting a renewed version of moral nominalism, revisionism asks whether and to what extent we can *really know in any given instance* if a particular choice or behavior can be understood to constitute the behavior identified and prohibited by the norm.

On such an account of human action, all choices and actions are irreducible to "kinds" of action. Consequently, the whole moral project, as conceived of by the Catholic moral tradition, in which the role of conscience is to apply appropriate moral norms to kinds of actions, is quietly discarded as out of touch with the "real" situation of individuals. For revisionist moral theologians, conscience still has a role—an enormous role, to be sure—but one quite removed from the Church's perennial understanding of conscience and prudence, especially as received from Thomas Aquinas.

Consequently, all norms are subject to adaptation and flexibility. And ultimately, it will be the (putatively) discerning individual who will (presumably "in conscience") decide what he should do. And that decision is not only conclusive; it *constitutes truth*—truth for that individual. Such a vision, we should note, rides on an account of truth as ultimately reducible to narrative; consequently, as Abigail Favale puts it succinctly, "because truth is just a story we tell ourselves, all self-told stories are true."[6]

To suggest that *all* moral norms should be subject to such adaptation and flexibility is not only to reduce the whole of moral normativity to moral *policy*, but also to suggest the nonexistence of exceptionless moral norms, a stance incompatible with perennial Catholic moral teaching.

Underlying this moral theological quagmire are, first of all, two problematic notions: a conception of conscience as *personal decision* and a dualistic notion of human freedom.

The view of conscience as personal decision conflates the genuine judgment of conscience (which can and should arise independently of one's decision-making capacity) with mere moral *opinion*. In the Catholic understanding of conscience—based firmly on the thought of Thomas Aquinas (who, in turn, it must be pointed out, was simply being a student of human psychology here)—conscience does not create moral norms; it is not literally autonomous, a law unto itself. Rather, conscience is the manifestation of human practical reason guiding an individual to be fully reasonable, to embrace and be harmonious with a perceived ordering of personal choices and actions, that most fully respects the integrity of the human goods involved and is most conducive to one's genuine flourishing and that of others.

Aquinas held that conscience, in the strict sense, was an act of human reason—a judgment—that can precede, accompany, or present itself subsequent to choice. Conscience is reason's awareness of a choice or action's harmony or disharmony with the kind of behavior that truly leads to our genuine well-being and flourishing. The genuine judgment of conscience stands before us, so to speak, independent of our feelings and opinions regarding our chosen actions.

In fact, a person might make "decisions" based on "opinions" about how to achieve the good without ever getting in touch with the genuine judgment of conscience on such matters. According to the contemporary view, conscience is essentially creative, autonomous, a law unto itself, settling personal moral matters by way of autonomous decision. Such a conception is simply incompatible with the anthropology of the human person that undergirds the Church's received moral teaching.

We cannot help but note that this faulty notion of conscience continues to go hand in hand with the older faulty notion of freedom and moral self-determination proposed by Proportionalist ethicists and rejected by *Veritatis Splendor*. To summarize that view briefly,

- Human freedom actually operates on two levels, one conscious—the state in which we make everyday choices—and the other deeper, transcending conscious awareness, wherein we find our true self-worth and determine ourselves as moral beings, where we have presumably made a "fundamental option" for or against God.

- Seemingly, however, on this account of freedom, and barring stark evidence to the contrary (such as having a zest for committing crimes against humanity), everyone's fundamental option is basically in the "right" direction from the get-go of one's moral life: the radical orientation of one's whole life is toward God, as evidenced by the collective whole of one's "right" moral choices in everyday life, the rightness of which is primarily assessed by the motives that inform them.

- Given this two-tiered understanding of personal freedom, a person can licitly, at times, *choose* what these theorists would term as "pre-moral," "physical," or "ontic" evils (such as abortion, adultery, euthanasia, and the like), albeit reluctantly and regrettably, and bring them about. However, if brought about for personally valid and substantial reasons, such choices and actions can be "right" moral options. Nor do these choices have an impact on the core or fundamental moral goodness—the fundamental option—of persons who, thus, operate as long as their choices are buoyed by right motivations and a careful moral calculus that has assured a greater net outcome of good consequences over evil or less desirable consequences in choosing and acting.

While *Veritatis Splendor* thoroughly excoriated this dualistic understanding of human freedom that separates choices and actions from one's fundamental option, those ideas remain very influential. There remains much resistance to John Paul II's insistence that Proportionalist anthropology introduces an unacceptable rift between faith, on the one hand, and the moral life, on the other:

> The relationship between faith and morality shines forth with all its brilliance in the *unconditional respect due to the insistent demands of the personal dignity of every man,* demands protected by those moral norms which prohibit without exception actions which are intrinsically evil. The universality and the immutability of the moral norm make manifest and at the same time serve to protect the personal dignity and inviolability of man, on whose face is reflected the splendor of God.[7]

And, as we saw from the outset, to abandon the truth of exceptionless moral norms is ultimately an affront to the dignity of the human person:

> The unacceptability of "teleological", "consequentialist" and "proportionalist" ethical theories, which deny the existence of negative moral norms regarding specific kinds of behavior, norms which are valid without exception, is confirmed in a particularly eloquent way by Christian martyrdom, which has always accompanied and continues to accompany the life of the Church even today.[8]

The "weight" of moral truth, its transcendence and eternal consequences, has been attested to by the martyrs. How can we not think, for example, of Saint Maria Gorretti and Saint Thomas More?

Genuine Pastoral Accompaniment and the Diakonia Veritatis

Called to evangelize a world of individuals who, for the most part, understand themselves as autonomous (not to say Cartesian) selves, when proposing the truths of Christian faith and morality, our efforts are easily perceived of as uncomfortably invasive, if not entirely threatening. At the basis of the disconnect between freedom and truth—a central concern of *Veritatis Splendor*—is a widespread culture of distrust-of-truth claims, especially absolute ones. As John Paul II noted about our times,

> There are signs of a widespread distrust of universal and absolute statements, especially among those who think that truth is born of consensus and not of a consonance between intellect and objective reality.[9]

For many, systems of thought that propose universal truths about the human person are not only suspect, but downright threatening. In today's Areopagus, the disciples of Jesus have to understand this. Does that mean we stop proposing a robust understanding of the truth of the human person? Of course not. But we have to make clear that in the end, truth is not just an idea because ideas can, in fact, seem threatening. Today, it is more urgent than ever for disciples of Jesus to courageously acknowledge not simply their "belief" that "the truth exists," but to give evidence that they have encountered the truth, and this truth is a Person. Christ endowed His Church with the Magisterium as a "diakonia" or service of Christian truth:

> It is her duty to serve humanity in different ways, but one way in particular imposes a responsibility of a quite special kind: the *diakonia of the truth*. This mission on the one hand makes the believing community a partner in humanity's shared struggle to arrive at truth; and on the other hand it obliges the believing community to proclaim the certitudes arrived at, albeit with a sense that every truth attained is but a step towards that fullness of truth which will appear with the final Revelation of God.[10]

In service to humanity, the Church's pastors, in communion with the successor of Peter, are charged with discerning the ideas of every age to determine whether they are compatible with the Word of God and with the deposit of divinely revealed truth. And as affirmed by the Second Vatican Council, the Magisterium is also competent to teach authoritatively on matters not only of faith, but faith and morals.[11] Yet, this is not a policing action. Rather, it is the way in which the Church accompanies humanity in the common search for truth:

This discernment, however, should not be seen as primarily negative, as if the Magisterium intended to abolish or limit any possible mediation. On the contrary, the Magisterium's interventions are intended above all to prompt, promote and encourage philosophical enquiry . . . [For] the Church knows that "the treasures of wisdom and knowledge" are hidden in Christ (*Col* 2:3) and therefore intervenes in order to stimulate philosophical enquiry, lest it stray from the path which leads to recognition of the mystery.[12]

Gerhard Cardinal Müller has beautifully highlighted that the Church's service of truth should, in fact, be motivated by the hope that every man and woman would discover the joy of *giving ourselves* to the Truth:

"The service to Christian truth which the Magisterium renders is thus for the benefit of the whole People of God called to enter the liberty of the truth revealed by God in Christ" (*Donum Veritatis*, 14). . . . [it] is ultimately a service of the continuing possibility of unreserved self-gift to that truth, and communion in that self-gift, which, as we have seen, is not a self-offering to an abstraction, but to the arms of the Father-Creator and the exigencies of His love, which is the basis for communion.[13]

In essentially rejecting the need for a Magisterium, in discarding the truth of objective moral norms, and the reality of intrinsically disordered acts, and in promoting a concept of conscience as an autonomous source of self-validating moral truths, revisionist moral theologians make a mockery of the witness of courageous men and women throughout the Church's history who gave their lives for moral truth.

*Genuine Pastoral Accompaniment and the
Principle of Gradualness*

As a consequence of the preceding problematic notions, some bishops have suggested that it can be possible for at least some of the baptized to remain validly (without consequence to their ultimate salvation) and in varying degrees *in communion* with the Church even when, in their lifestyle choices (their "conscience decisions"), they openly reject the Church's perennial moral teachings on marriage, cohabitation, premarital sex, and sexual activity between persons of the same sex.

To be clear, we are not talking about persons who might engage in such behaviors in a state of invincible ignorance (which the Church's moral tradition naturally understands can attenuate and even eliminate personal responsibility); the idea here is that persons would knowingly engage in such behaviors acknowledging the inconsistency of such behaviors with Church teaching, even that they are gravely sinful. The further idea is that, in response, *the Church would somehow find a way to affirm some degree of soundness in their moral status, and "good standing" or communion, with the Church.*

To arrive at such a proposition involves, in addition to the preceding notions, a problematic understanding of personal moral progress. Specifically, it requires taking more than a bit of theological license with a principle of Catholic moral teaching normally referred to as the "law of gradualness." As a moral principle, the law of gradualness became fully part of the moral theological lexicon with the publication of *Familiaris Consortio* (in a paragraph that includes an internal quote of a homily Pope Saint John Paul II delivered at the close of the sixth Synod of Bishops, October 25, 1980):

And so what is known as "the law of gradualness" or step-by-step advance cannot be identified with "gradualness of the law," as if there were different degrees or forms of precept in God's law for different individuals and situations. In God's plan, all husbands and wives are called in marriage to holiness, and this lofty vocation is fulfilled to the extent that the human person is able to respond to God's command with serene confidence in God's grace and in his or her own will.[14]

Though not offering a precise formulation of the principle of gradualness, John Paul II, in the same exhortation, points to the proper Christian context that forms the framework within which this moral principle is to be properly understood:

What is needed is a continuous, permanent conversion which, while requiring an interior detachment from every evil and an adherence to good in its fullness, is brought about concretely in steps which lead us ever forward. Thus, a dynamic process develops, one which advances gradually with the progressive integration of the gifts of God and the demands of His definitive and absolute love in the entire personal and social life of man. Therefore, an educational growth process is necessary, in order that individual believers, families and peoples, even civilization itself, by beginning from what they have already received of the mystery of Christ, may patiently be led forward, arriving at a richer understanding and a fuller integration of this mystery in their lives.[15]

Hence, the principle of gradualness, properly understood, has its origin in the very reality of human psycho-moral development. As in most areas of human development, so too in the moral sphere, maturity manifests itself through a gradual process—"steps"—toward an ever-deeper appropriation of right moral behavior as instantiated in concrete choices and actions. In the Christian context, it articulates the gradual nature of conversion. Genuine conversion places us necessarily on a course that *intends* steady progress—notwithstanding human weakness and occasional moral failures—toward an ever more consistent and holistic embrace of the truth of Christ's moral teaching.

But it is vitally important to understand, as noted in section 34 of *Familiaris Consortio*, that the principle of gradualness does not imply that either the convert or the Church should craft and validate individualized and autonomous moral norms "as if there were different degrees or forms of precept in God's law for different individuals and situations." That would constitute the very perversion of the law of gradualness to which John Paul II refers—namely, the "gradualness of the law." Converts to the faith are to be led and assisted in appropriating the new moral requirements of life in Christ in progressive steps of gradual conversion and exigency, assuring them of God's mercy, presence, and grace, safeguarding against their discouragement, accompanying them in a step-by-step renewal of life *but without diminishing the full import of the moral requirements.*

The "Both-And" Approach: Speaking the Truth in Love

If evangelization of such a culture is to be effective, we must understand that it is incumbent upon us to present moral truths, but to do so in a manner that constitutes *an attractive and compelling alternative* to the modern ethos of hyper-focused individualism. We are called to present a vision of Christian moral living that is compelling and attractive, not off-putting and threatening.

The error that overzealous disciples can make is to be too insistent from the get-go on moral norms and the push to bring others to normative living. If we insist too rigidly on taking a "moral truth approach" or a "moral norm approach" that is overbearing and short on listening, on a sense of graduality and accompaniment, our approach will often only be perceived as "moralizing." It will also come across as "intolerance," and many of our brothers and sisters will be turned off to our message.

How, then, to present this attractive and compelling alternative that our experience of Jesus and His perennial teaching—including moral teaching—in the Church provides us? We might call it a *beauty-first* approach. How does that work? To borrow an analogy from Bishop Robert Barron: When a child begins to show interest in baseball, should dad start by explaining the infield fly rule? Or would he have a much better shot at nourishing that child's interest in baseball by starting with something else—something attractive and beautiful in its own right: presenting the child with his own old leather glove that he wore when he was a kid, and taking the child to their first MLB game at the stadium?[16]

As the analogy illustrates, the way it seems we can best reach our brothers and sisters is not by way of what we are most inclined to do, or most used to doing, which is leading with claims about moral truth. On the contrary, we often need to set that aside—for a time—and take another avenue, another approach, one that first emphasizes the beauty and attractiveness of the Christian moral life. Is that not also how, in the first three centuries, Christianity prevailed? As sociologist and historian Rodney Stark has pointed out, in its treatment of women, slaves, newborns, foreigners, and the sick, in the peaceful response to violence, Christianity was a bright and beautiful reality in an ugly and violent world. This—*its inherent, attractive, and compelling beauty*—brings Christianity from an outlying small and obscure religious sect to becoming the religion of the Roman Empire.[17]

This brings us to the heart of what it means to "[speak] the truth in love" (Eph 4:15).[18] The very "love" referenced in that verse—*agape*-love for our post-modern neighbor—requires us to *package and deliver* that truth carefully. Truth can be spoken and explained; it can also be *shown and its beauty manifested without argumentation*. There is a difference between telling and manifesting, just as there is a great difference between *convicting someone and convincing someone*.

I believe we live in an age when genuine Christian *agape*-love compels us to point our brothers and sisters toward the beauty of the Truth. Oftentimes, in order to speak the truth in love, we must first *show the splendor* of the truth in love, communicated by beautiful people, beautiful souls, who radiate joy, not scowls, not axes to grind, not anger and bitterness, but joy.

So, in engaging the culture, in engaging the autonomous Cartesian self who disagrees with us on abortion, gay unions, contraception, and a host of other issues, let us not start with the infield fly rule. Let us start with the beauty of a green, grassy, freshly trimmed infield at the stadium. Notwithstanding the evident and ever-growing complexity of the manner in which the Church attempts to communicate truth to a post-modern secular culture, we pray that we all may be endowed with the patience necessary to accompany our brothers and sisters, applying the principle of gradualness. This does not require of us to validate behavior that is incompatible with human flourishing or to embrace a false understanding of conscience. It does require of us, in addition to having loads of patience, a docility to the Holy Spirit, the exercise of pastoral prudence, and a genuine discernment of a person's situation. Ultimately, it will also require of us the courage, when the moment is right, to speak the truth in love. All this is entailed in the *diakonia veritatis*.

Notes

1. John Paul II, *Veritatis Splendor* (1993), sec. 3, emphasis added.
2. *Veritatis Splendor*, sec. 90, emphasis added.
3. See my "Self-Originating Source of Valid Moral Claims or Witness to Moral Truth?" *Nova et Vetera* (forthcoming). The exact origin of the term "revisionist" is debatable. James Keenan, SJ—himself a prominent revisionist moral theologian—uses the term with some regularity. My use reflects his own. Broadly speaking, the term refers to moral theologians of the twentieth century who endeavored to contribute to a reform of manualist moral theology. Keenan identifies as "revisionist" in a narrower sense those moral theologians who made the concept of "fundamental option" central to their moral systems, among them Louis Janssens, Josef Fuchs, and the later Bernard Häring. See James Keenan, "Virtue, Grace and the Early Revisionists of the Twentieth Century," *Studies in Christian Ethics* 23, no. 4: 365–380.
4. Raymond Leo Cardinal Burke, "Discipline and Doctrine: Law in the Service of Truth and Love," *What We Need Now*, https://whatweneednow.substack.com/p/discipline-and-doctrine-law-in-the?utm_source=substack&utm_medium=email.
5. Francis, Apostolic Journey of His Holiness Pope Francis to Portugal on the Occasion of the XXXVII World Youth Day (August 6, 2023), author's own translation. For English version, see https://www.vatican.va/content/francesco/en/speeches/2023/august/documents/20230806-portogallo-voloritorno.html.
6. Abigail Favale, *The Genesis of Gender* (San Francisco: Ignatius Press, 2022), 31.
7. *Veritatis Splendor*, sec. 90.
8. *Veritatis Splendor*, sec. 90.
9. John Paul II, *Fides et Ratio* (1998), sec. 56.
10. *Fides et Ratio*, sec. 2. See also John Paul II, *Redemptor Hominis* (1979), sec. 19.
11. "Although the individual bishops do not enjoy the prerogative of infallibility, they nevertheless proclaim Christ's doctrine infallibly whenever, even though dispersed through the world, but still maintaining the bond of communion among themselves and with the successor of Peter, and authentically teaching matters of faith and morals, they are in agreement on one position as definitively to be held. This is even more clearly verified when, gathered together in an ecumenical council, they are teachers and judges of faith and morals for the universal Church, whose definitions must be adhered to with the submission of faith." Vatican II, *Lumen Gentium* (1964), sec. 25.
12. *Fides et Ratio*, sec. 51.

13. Cardinal Gerhard L. Müller, "Donum Veritatis: The Contribution of the Congregation for the Doctrine of the Faith to the Theological Enterprise," *Nova et Vetera,* English Edition, 13, no. 3 (2015): 642.

14. John Paul II, *Familiaris Consortio* (1981), sec. 34.

15. *Familiaris Consortio,* sec. 9.

16. See John L. Allen, Jr., "Barron Muses on Evangelization, Bob Dylan and the Infield Fly Rule" in *Crux* (October 31, 2017), https://cruxnow.com/interviews/2017/10/barron-muses-evangelization-bob-dylan-infield-fly-rule.

17. See Rodney Stark, *The Rise of Christianity: A Sociologist Reconsiders History* (Princeton: Princeton University Press, 2020).

18. This quote is from the New Revised Standard version of the Bible.

Veritatis Splendor: A Bishop's Response

Earl K. Fernandes

My Dear Friends in Christ, I am very grateful for the invitation to participate in this seminar. Allow me to thank Deacon James Keating for his gracious invitation, as well as Dr. Anderson, Dr. Rath, Father Billy, and Father Berg. Section 29 of *Veritatis Splendor* invites moral theologians to deepen and perfect their labors in carrying out the renewal in moral theology called for by the Council. I must admit that it is with some trepidation that I write, following papers and presentations of such high caliber. While my doctoral degree is in moral theology, it has been years since I actively engaged in the field. I miss seminary work; and hearing Father Billy speak, I was reminded how privileged I was to learn from him. Seminary is a privileged time for learning, and it is my privilege to be with you.

In these remarks, I do not intend to offer a systematic response to what I have heard during these days; rather, I hope to offer some insight from the perspective of a bishop as to what expectations I might have with respect to the clergy as moral teachers and guides for living the Christian way of life, commenting upon the relevant points of what has been written.

I would like to begin with some general observations about *Veritatis Splendor*. First, while much of the commentary on the encyclical and the critique of the encyclical when it was first issued focused on the second part of the encyclical (which included statements regarding absolute moral norms, intrinsically evil acts, and critiques of proportionalism and its variants), I believe that two dimensions of the encyclical were, and remain, grossly overlooked—the Christological foundations of morality and the ecclesial and pastoral nature of Christian moral life. Hence, this seminar, with its emphasis on the pastor's task, is one way of demonstrating the ecclesial and pastoral nature of Christian moral life.

As a bishop who has charge over priests and who is concerned with the pastor's task of being an effective instrument of the New Evangelization, I would say one basic expectation for the clergy is that they nurture their relationship with Jesus Christ, to whom the priest is configured and who ultimately serves as the Teacher *par excellence*, and that they remember that they are men of the Church, ordained for service of the Church, of the Holy People of God. When one is advising penitents or giving counsel to parishioners, the Word spoken must be Jesus Christ and the norms proposed by the Church. There are not two standards of morality: one for the rich and one for the poor, one for the holy and one for the fragile. The same Gospel—Good News—is proposed to all, yet it will be the pastor's task to accompany the pilgrim on his or her journey to rise to the greatness to which the Christian is called.

Shortly after I became Bishop, I went to a parish in my diocese, and a couple came out of Mass and asked: "Bishop, do you remember us?" I said, "Yes. You're Frank and Jessica."

Now, I had not seen the couple for fifteen years. They were practicing Catholics and married in the Church. They had tried to have children but without success. They had gone to see their parish priest about in-vitro fertilization (IVF), and the priest explained Church teaching, and they were saddened. The woman's father, who was also Catholic, remembered me from my first parish and told his daughter to check with me because I was young and interested in medical ethics. Maybe, he thought, she would get a more favorable answer.

I met with the couple, who genuinely wanted to do the right thing, and walked them through *Dignitas Personae*, after which they began to realize they were not going to get the answer her father had suggested. I explained Church teaching, spoke to them about the loss of embryonic life, and also spoke about the expense of the treatment. The wife, bursting into tears, said, "But we can afford it!" But I answered, "Imagine you were a poor couple. What would you do? You would probably accept this cross from God and turn to Him in your grief. There are not two standards: one for the rich and one for the poor." The husband began to shake his head, acknowledging what I was saying.

I said, "Look, I wouldn't be a good spiritual father to you if I lied to you or didn't give you the full teaching. Take a copy of this document. Read it, and pray about it. Call me if you have any questions. I'm not going to be looking over your shoulder; but if you trust God, everything will be okay."

Fifteen years later, they are happily married. They did not choose IVF or adoption. They simply lived their faith, carried their cross, and grew in holiness day by day, supporting one another. Recently, they invited me to their home, and I explained that I had never forgotten them because I saw in them a couple who wanted to be faithful, even if it was not easy.

Recently, Archbishop Fernandez, the new prefect of the Dicastery for the Doctrine of the Faith, suggested that after *Veritatis Splendor*, theologians became afraid and lost some of their creativity. Within the larger context, he wondered why we were not producing great theologians, as the last century had in persons like Rahner, Balthasar, de Lubac, Congar, etc. The same, he mused, could be said of liberation theology. Of course, the theological greats of the last century were particularly gifted, having a thorough knowledge of languages, philosophy, theology, and culture; and they could produce great theology, even during a period in which they had to take the oath against Modernism. Theological reflection and creativity need not be stifled by fear; rather, *"perfect love drives out fear"* (1 Jn 4:18, emphasis added). Thus, we must be serious about deepening our knowledge through study but also our love of Christ and His Church, guided by the Holy Spirit, if we are to truly bring about the desired renewal of moral theology.

Second, we must properly comprehend that the manualist tradition, which dominated prior to the Council, led to the understanding of morality as a legalistic imposition of precepts. *Veritatis Splendor* asserts, in contrast, that "Love and life according to the Gospel, cannot be thought of first and foremost as a kind of precept"[1]; and, secondly, that "Christian morality consists, in the simplicity of the Gospel, in following Jesus Christ, in abandoning oneself to Him, in letting oneself be transformed by his grace and renewed by His mercy, gifts which come to us in the living communion of the Church."[2]

We can think of Benedict XVI's first encyclical, *Deus Caritas Est*, where he wrote in the first paragraph that "Being a Christian is not a result of an ethical choice or a lofty idea; rather, it is the result of an encounter with an event or a Person, who opens up new horizons and gives our life a decisive direction."[3]

To be able to recognize the original perspective of morality, it seems necessary to put oneself in the perspective of the acting person, who determines himself in and through his freely chosen acts. This is why Dr. Rath's presentation seems to me to be so important: our chosen acts affect our character—who we are and who we are becoming. They can destroy the bond of charity in the heart and give a decisive direction to our path—a direction that does not lead to heaven or happiness, *or* they can lead to conversion and Paradise.

It is important to understand what we are freely choosing and, as clergy, to be able to clearly distinguish the object, the intention, and the surrounding circumstances of an act. The circumstances can help us determine a suitable penance or a remedy to help a person continue his or her deeper conversion to Christ or to help us make judgments about a person's moral responsibility or, if nothing else, help us to empathize. Our individual actions bear witness to our longing for the Good, for God Himself, the ultimate aim of our moral actions.

If Christian morality consists principally in following Christ, then it seems to me that a central thrust of *Veritatis Splendor* and of our pastoral task is to recover the theological dimension of the Christian moral life, since it bears witness to the primacy of grace in our free response to God's initiative, to the Christological form of the gift that shapes our response, and to the ecclesial character of our own existence in Christ.

Ecclesial incorporation into Christ through the means of grace is at the very heart of the moral dynamism of the faithful.

Theologians such as Henri de Lubac reflected on the social dimensions of the Sacraments of the Church and of Baptism as the means of incorporation into the Body of Christ. The section on morality in the *Catechism* is rightly called "Moral Life in Christ." Hence, what was particularly striking to me about Father Billy's essay is not merely what conscience is but *how* conscience is formed. That is, conscience is formed not only by reason but by Scripture, Tradition, and the Magisterium of the Church. To rightly form and inform one's conscience, one needs to have an ecclesial sensibility, for it is the Church who rightly interprets Scripture, who teaches truths flowing from Scripture and the natural law, who guides, under the influence of the Holy Spirit, the whole body of believers. Indeed, the lives of believers, especially those of the saints, including people like Thomas More or the Ugandan martyrs, more than the subjective experience of one individual, contribute to the formation of conscience.

In July 2023, I was at Benedictine College in Atchison, Kansas for the Courage International Conference. There were men and women who struggled with same-sex attraction yet earnestly desired to live a chaste life. Theirs was a beautiful struggle, and they longed for accompaniment. They understood and accepted Church teaching and wanted to live their faith in the Church and to be faithful. I admired them.

They reminded me of a man whom I knew when I was a parish priest who also struggled with same-sex attraction; he came for Mass, for confession, and for spiritual direction. I admired his courage and his persistence in wanting to be chaste. He would not give up. Eventually, I was transferred to work at the Nunciature and returned to my diocese only for ordinations that year. I saw the man on the steps of the cathedral, and we spontaneously embraced. I admired him so much because he was willing, time and again, to get back on the road—to continue his faith journey. Never once did he ask for the Church to change her teaching because he firmly believed it was true. All he asked for was God's grace and someone to help him to abide in that grace.

The New Evangelization:
The Context of the Renewal of Moral Theology

One of the principal tasks of pastors is to proclaim the Gospel of Jesus Christ. Last year, when I attended "Baby Bishops' School," as they call it, Cardinal Farrell and two laywomen, serving as secretaries in the Dicastery for Family, Laity, and Life, told us that we should not apologize for Church teaching on the family, marriage, and life because it is truly Good News, necessary for the New Evangelization.

Veritatis Splendor proposes that the Church can "offer everyone the answer which comes from the truth about Jesus Christ and His Gospel,"[4] that she can make possible "the encounter with Christ,"[5] and that God has willed this encounter for His Church,[6] an encounter that alone can fully satisfy the desire of the human heart. The question of morality (and its renewal) can be situated within the challenge of the New Evangelization, a challenge that the Church has been called to confront from its origins.[7]

Nearly forty years ago, Cardinal Paul Poupard undertook a study of the state of morality, which he discovered to be in a state of crisis, a crisis that has only worsened over the last four decades. He noted that there was a questioning of traditional values and a rejection of an ethical code having an external reference point in favor of a *radical subjectivization of morality*.

The crisis was not merely created by a repudiation of moral norms taught by the Magisterium but *the imperviousness of the conscience of so many of the faithful to the teaching of the Church*. The legalization of abortion, euthanasia and physician-assisted suicide, as well as the redefinition of marriage in the civil code, and the acceptance and promotion of many of these practices by mainstream Christian denominations has contributed to this imperviousness.

The crisis is not merely one of the practicing of the faith, but it appears to be more profound. It is a question of the judgment about good and evil. It is the claim that individual conscience is the sole and autonomous judge deciding what is good and what is evil. The conscience is becoming increasingly emancipated from "ecclesial communion." Before the 2012 *ad limina* visits, the American cardinals were consulted about the most serious challenges to the Church in the United States; Cardinal George suggested that one of those challenges was that people have lost the sense of the Church as Mother and Teacher. They view her as a bureaucratic institution and not their family. In the progression toward an "autonomous conscience," we observe that there is a weakening relationship with the Church herself.

So, how did we get here? Beyond the doctrinal points, *Veritatis Splendor* attends to two deep fissures in the roots of moral theology, which continue to recur: the breaking of the bond between freedom and truth and of that between faith and morals.[8] The first is a philosophical problem because it does not maintain any possible link between reason and universal permanent truth, abandoning freedom to subjective arbitrariness, and leads to a contractual understanding of public morality. The second unhinges the unity and totality of the act of faith, precipitating a rupture between faith and morality, suggesting a pluralism of views on significant moral issues that leads to division and polarization within the Church.

Already in the last century, Heidegger observed that technology was developing at a rapid pace and was in no way neutral; rather, it reshaped our vision of reality and the conception of human freedom.[9] Pope Benedict warned of this in *Caritas in Veritate*, and Pope Francis did in *Laudato Si*. The technical aspect of reason is overwhelming the philosophical and sapiential aspects. Technological advancement, including the development of Artificial Intelligence, is rapidly outpacing philosophical reflection; but as philosophy and ethics attempt to offer a framework, the mentality of the people living through this rapid change is being shaped. Pope Francis has said, "We live not so much in an epoch of change as in a change of epoch."[10]

A prevailing concept is the denial of the idea that there is any truth about a created thing that is to be respected *and* the related concept that everything can, thus, be manipulated without limits, which we see today in the manipulation of the body in the ambit of gender reassignment or in the transhumanism movement. If being in the world does not come from a creative act of God, if it does not express His wise and sapiential plan but derives from chance, then everything is open to manipulation.

Moral values become not the fruit of knowledge but of subjective feelings, emotions, or arbitrary choices. Thus, in the arena of discursive ethics in a pluralistic society, ethics is concerned not with what is true or with what is good, since it is impossible to know these things; rather, ethics is concerned with establishing procedural rules by which everyone participates and is respected as a participant, but without any judgment about the content of morality or without any critical investigation of the rational foundations of positions.

Pastors, therefore, need to recognize this changed, technological environment and its effects on people's patterns of thinking and judgments as they accompany their parishioners. Pastoral attention must also be given to the religiously non-affiliated or so-called "nones" because if belief in God is absent or only vague, it becomes hard to establish that persons have inherent dignity or that a sapiential plan, in fact, exists, a plan (with its norms) that reason can apprehend.

The second rupture is that between faith and morality. As the Christian universe fragmented, it became impossible to construct a social coexistence on a religious basis. Philosophers and humanists turned to reason as the sole source of universal moral evidence. We can see how far we have moved even from their perspective. Immanuel Kant held that while Christian morality is the expression of truly universal ethical demands, valid for all people for all times, it is necessary to detach it from every historical reference, including the person of Jesus. He desired to affirm the absoluteness of morality, while detaching it from the ethics of faith; reason, therefore, could apprehend its duties and responsibilities and would be kept within limits by the law.

In his book *After Virtue*, Alasdair McIntyre contended that while we used words like "conscience" and "virtues" from a previously Christian era, we had principally forgotten what morality was all about and we needed to recover an "ethic of virtue," which necessarily involved not only the question "What must I do?" but also: "Who am I? Who ought I become?" What attitudes and actions lead me to what I ought become? What kind of community can lead me to become the person I am ideally called to become?

I believe that *Veritatis Splendor* is concerned with these fundamental questions. How does what I do affect who I am? How does who I am affect what I do? These are pertinent questions, especially for those who purport to be followers of Jesus and members of His Church. The encyclical letter wants to address these two fissures and to offer moral life a home within the community of believers. We can all easily realize how much of our task as pastors remains before us.

Making Connections: Healing the Breach

In *Veritatis Splendor*, John Paul II spends a significant amount of time meditating on the story of the rich young man who asks: "What good must I do to have eternal life?" (Mt 19:16) Jesus responds by asking, "Why do you ask me about the good? There is only One who is good" (Mt 19:17).

Jesus wants to invite the man to probe the deepest roots of his question. The question of morality is not one, first and foremost, about norms, as important as those are; rather, it is about a yearning for the Absolute Good. The good to which we aspire ultimately is God Himself. This aspirational good is always something more than that which we can do. The good has a religious and salvific character to it. Nevertheless, as Dr. Rath pointed out, actions (what we do) matter. Actions bear witness to the longing for the infinite and help us realize this longing symbolically.

The fissure introduced by Kant can be overcome by proposing a morality of happiness and of blessed fulfillment rather than one of duties and obligations. The human person has impressed within himself or herself an orientation toward God and a desire for the true good. Reason attempts to discover the originating law of being, that is, the natural law, which is not in opposition to freedom.

The next connection that must be "re-made" is the bond between faith and morality. As I said previously, the fundamental word, which John Paul II uses,[11] which Benedict XVI mentioned, and which Pope Francis never ceases to use is "encounter." When we reflect on the rich young man, it is noteworthy that he walks away sad. He has had this wonderful encounter, yet because of his many possessions and his attachment to them, he cannot follow; he cannot set out on a great adventure, despite his attraction to Jesus.

Ethics is born of an encounter in which one perceives that the promise of blessed self-fulfillment can be realized in a human way. If moral dynamism is the dynamism of love, love is provoked by beauty. Christ is the Good Shepherd, the Beautiful Shepherd. His love is beautiful.

The Role of Beauty

Mark's Gospel says that Jesus looked upon the rich young man. His gaze was one of love. He awakened desire in the man, but the man still had to choose to follow. Here, I wish to digress on the subject of beauty because Father Billy pointed out that our conscience does not see things perfectly due to the effects of Original Sin, and Dr. Anderson pointed out the need for *claritas*, which is a property of truth that connects the true and beautiful and is a transcendent property of beauty.

The ancients, in reflecting on beauty, spoke of *integritas, harmonia, and claritas* and connected these aspects with wholeness or the perfection of form. My friend Dr. Mary Catherine Levri recently taught a course on beauty, and she used Ann Astell's book *Eating Beauty: The Eucharist and the Spiritual Arts of the Middle Ages*. Astell argues that the main spiritualities of the Middle Ages (the Franciscans, the Cistercians, the Dominicans, and later, the Jesuits) receive their charisms from Jesus in the Eucharist. These spiritualities or ways of holiness serve to restore the God-given beauty of the fallen world, to appreciate the beauty of God in created things. Nourished and transformed by the Eucharist, the saints restore the beauty of the world in and through the radiation of the beautiful virtues that they have received from the Lord. Beauty is primarily connected with sanctity and commitment to holiness of life.

In the Eucharist, we receive the whole Christ and observe that the deformity of His Passion and the glory of His Resurrection are held together in His form as slave and in His form as God. Christ goes beyond the ancient concept of beauty in His self-giving love, which includes His suffering, and He transforms us. The lives of the saints include the "deformity of the Lord" as well as His glory. We bear the sufferings of Christ in our bodies, even as we experience a foretaste of the pledge of future glory.

Why this digression? I believe that the *ars celebrandi* of the Liturgy is important for the experience of beauty and for the transformation of hearts and minds. In light of what is celebrated and the One who is received, the Christian faithful can experience the beauty of the Lord's love. Thus, I think the decoration of the church, the worthiness of the vestments, the thoughtful selection of chants and hymns all contribute to the encounter with the Lord that allows us to experience His love, which precedes our desire but which subsequently increases our desire for life with Him and in Him, now and in eternity.

Jesus gazed on the rich young man with love. This gaze is also important for pastors when encountering penitents. To look upon them with love, to listen with love is to affirm that they matter. The dispensation of grace is not mechanical, and the pastoral style—the gaze of mercy—is critical to effective accompaniment and to the Christian way of life.

Veritatis Splendor points out that Christianity is "not simply a set of propositions to be accepted with intellectual assent" but is a "truth to be lived out."[12] It must engage one's whole life. It is one thing to present right teaching, but it is another to express the truth in love, with a gaze of tenderness and mercy. Christianity, ultimately, is a concrete way of living. The Christian, having been gazed upon with love, feels valued and recognizes the truth of Jesus's words, "I am the way and the truth and the life" (Jn 14:6).

Thus, in the confessional or in the office, the parishioner ought to experience from his or her pastor the gaze of Christ, the patience of Christ, and the comfort of Christ the Physician, the Merciful Redeemer. Morality must have a Christological foundation, not merely in theory or in the abstract, but in concrete gestures. Again, *Veritatis Splendor* notes that "Christ is the Beginning who, having taken on human nature, definitively illumines it in its constitutive elements and in its dynamism of charity toward God and neighbor."[13]

In the encounter with Christ, the person discovers his own weakness and fragility, as did Peter in the story of the haul of great fish or when he denied Christ three times; but, at the same time, he also discovers Christ's unwillingness to abandon him. Section 103 of *Veritatis Splendor*, I believe, is the core of the encyclical:

> *Only in the mystery of Christ's Redemption do we discover the "concrete" possibilities of man.* "It would be a very serious error to conclude... that the Church's teaching is essentially only an 'ideal' which must then be adapted, proportioned, graduated to the so-called concrete possibilities of man, according to a 'balancing of the goods in question'. But what are the 'concrete possibilities of man'? And of *which* man are we speaking? Of man *dominated* by lust or of man *redeemed by Christ*? This is what is at stake: the *reality* of Christ's redemption. *Christ has redeemed us*! This means that he has given us the possibility of realizing *the entire* truth of our being; he has set our freedom free from the *domination* of concupiscence. And if redeemed man still sins, this is not due to an imperfection of Christ's redemptive act, but to man's will not to avail himself of the grace which flows from that act. God's command is of course proportioned to man's capabilities; but to the capabilities of the man to whom the Holy Spirit has been given; of the man who, though he has fallen into sin, can always obtain pardon and enjoy the presence of the Holy Spirit."[14]

The gaze of mercy and love involves conveying the idea, through concrete actions and gestures, that the person before us, with God's grace, can realize the truth of his or her being. This is what "accompaniment," a term used by Pope Francis repeatedly, means. This is why Father Berg's intervention is so important.

Gradualness of Law and the Law of Gradualness: Authentic Accompaniment

One of the problems with the Church today can be illustrated by the so-called gradualness of law and the law of gradualness. To help us better understand the difference between gradualness of law and the law of gradualness, let us take an example from sports, pole vaulting specifically. If a pole vaulter repeatedly fails, someone might say, "Well, for you, we are going to lower the bar." The vaulter makes it over the low bar, gets a pat on the back, a participation trophy, and is sent on his or her way. This is gradualness of law as it pertains to faith, lowering the high standards of Christians, believing that the norms are impossible to be followed or lived.

Another option, however, after repeated failures to make it over the bar is for the coach to help the vaulter. The coach might notice that the vaulter's footwork and stride is off, and so the coach offers a few pointers. The vaulter is closer in the next attempt even if he is not successful. The coach then suggests another technique for planting the pole, while maintaining the now-learned skill of having the right stride. This time, the vaulter almost makes it over the bar. The coach then offers words of encouragement and suggests some additional strength training. Finally, the vaulter makes a solid effort, runs well, plants, pushes, and sails over the bar. It was a difficult task, but with accompaniment, a seemingly impossible height was attained. This describes the law of gradualness—with small steps, some coaching or accompaniment, and with words and encouragement, a new discipline and skill is acquired that allows for success in the spiritual life. The steps and improvements were small and happened gradually over time, but they happened, nonetheless.

Today, many moralists emphasize the primacy of charity. It is now more necessary than ever to understand that authentic charity demands truth, and that morality demands witnessing to Christ, even as the martyrs did. There is a great deal of moral confusion today, both within and outside the Church. To recognize the truth is fundamental, but it is not enough. It is the duty of pastors to help the faithful to grow to full stature in Christ and to continue their journey of faith, even with occasional falls, with the assurance that they are not alone in their journey.

Recognizing how fragile and weak people are and that the conscience is somewhat dulled, it is necessary to distinguish between gradualness of law, which reduces the law to a mere ideal, and the law of gradualness, which is understood as progress on the journey toward perfection.

What we observe today is a dichotomy between official Church doctrine and the concrete living of morality by many Christians. Some even speak of a true "moral schism," latent but, nevertheless, real. The personal conscience of the faithful does not accept any longer the normative, binding moral teachings of the Church. Doctrine alone no longer convinces; its demands are held as unreasonable or exorbitant; or while doctrines are true in theory, they are, practically speaking, impossible to live concretely in daily life. Those perennial moral norms, particularly in the area of sexual morality, including those regarding divorce and remarriage, contraception, masturbation, fornication, and sodomy, are now routinely rejected, and, we might add, not even considered in the moral calculus by many.

The temptation of pastors is simply not to address the issues, to leave them at the level of the private, the conscience of the faithful. The temptation is great because of a fear of backlash from parishioners, the loss of collections, a further dwindling of those in the pews, the media attention, etc. By clergy never addressing the issue, not only do the faithful never hear Church teaching, but there is a tacit acceptance of certain practices. Last year, we celebrated Safe Haven Sunday in my diocese. It was a Sunday to address the difficult issue of pornography and the related issue of human trafficking. I recorded a homily that was shown in every parish. I did not use the word "pornography," but everyone understood what I was talking about.

I used another sports analogy and spoke of the Cincinnati Bengals, who were perennial "cellar dwellers." They were terrible year after year and believed that they would lose, but then they got a new quarterback, Joe Burrow, and won a few games; but he got injured. The next year, he came back from injury, and they began to work together as a team and won a few games in a row. Little by little, they believed that they did not always have to lose; victory was possible. That year, they made it to the Super Bowl.

With pornography, many people feel that they have been defeated and that they must give in to temptation. It has reached pandemic proportions and is destroying families, yet no one ever wants to address it or offer individuals and families the tools they need to heal and to flourish again in freedom. We do not do our people a service by remaining silent. Of course, we have to be prudent in our speech and sensitive to people's conditions, but just as a doctor cannot ignore an illness, so too we, as pastors, cannot ignore the wounds of the flock and the flock's desire to get well. Such health will normally be achieved gradually.

The idea of the law of gradualness is to take the demands of morality seriously, connecting doctrine and practice, if Christianity, in the end, is really about living the newness of life in Christ. Still, we must acknowledge trends in theology that have contributed to gradualness of law.

Fifty years ago, Karl Rahner proposed the idea of evolving stages of conscience. One must admit the possibility that in our secularized society, a member of the faithful might theoretically recognize the existence of an official moral teaching of the Church but may not be successful in recognizing it as valid and normative for himself or herself in conscience. It might be information, but there is no existential recognition of the norm. Rahner held that the concrete existential level of acting is not exhaustively reached by objective norms and can only be intuited subjectively. He also held that the universal law cannot be applied mechanically to an individual case but only through the existential mediation of conscience and the gradualness of its phases of maturation.

Bernard Haring emerged from the era of morality understood as a prohibition of individual acts, which thereby controlled the freedom of the person, something he characterized as a hallmark of the pre-Conciliar Church. Morality could be understood as a series of normative ideals proposed to conscience but which does not substitute for an individual's creativity in formulating concrete judgments. The mature Christian is called to receive the fundamental orientations taught by the Magisterium but not necessarily the concrete normative determinations. Gradualness for Haring consisted in recognizing the primacy of the creative conscience of the subject that determines the path for growth. The Church would then propose prophetic ideals more than specific actions that the individual would have to adopt in his concrete journey.

Alain You, a French Benedictine, proposed an idea of gradualness by which the norm indicates the true good to be reached, and while there is a certain acceptance that the norm could not be immediately reached, a dynamic process could be put in place that would create the conditions by which the norm could be observed in the future. Thus, individual acts do not matter as much as the dynamic that leads to the eventual fulfillment of the norm. You extended the idea of gradualness not only to the positive commandments (growth toward the good) but also toward the negative commandments, speaking of a gradual distancing from evil.

We see these strains of thought present in our day, with a false contra-position between law and conscience, between the objective and subjective plane. Ultimately, all these perspectives, whether they admit or not, understand the moral life in a legalistic way. Something is good because it is commanded and evil because it is prohibited. Law is, thus, seen as a limit to the freedom of the subject and an enemy to his or her free will.

But the exactly opposite axiom is true: Something is commanded because it is good, and it is prohibited because it is evil. The moral norm is an expression of an awareness of the good of the person in relationship to a specific action. The negative norms indicate that a certain way of acting goes against the truth of the person and of love. To violate these moral norms is to act contrary to the good of the person.

These proposals also tend toward subjectivism to defend the person against the excesses of the law, thereby making the individual person/subject the measure of the law. But this approach closes the subject within his own proper measure and does not permit him to listen to those voices coming from outside (such as those from the Church or the lives of the saints), which would be the true measure. Moreover, if left to our own devices and our subjective judgments, to achieve "fulfillment," we would be practicing a form of Pelagianism, condemned by Pope Francis in *Gaudete et Exsultate*.

In contrast to the gradualness of law, there is the law of gradualness, which John Paul II proposed at the conclusion of the Synod for the Family and which appears in sections 9 and 34 of *Familiaris Consortio*, but which would certainly be presumed in *Veritatis Splendor*. The precepts of the law are not arbitrary but the truth that expresses the demands of the good of the person. Authentic pedagogy demands that from the beginning, one accept the normative and binding character, for every phase of growth, of the law of God. The precept permits the recognition of sin and the necessity of distancing oneself from it for an authentic conversion.

Jesus, the Good Shepherd, demonstrated this type of pedagogy. He did not come to abolish the law but to fulfill it. He deepened the morality proposed by Moses and later, by the Pharisees, exhorting His disciples to go beyond the mere external observances of the law to interior conversion.

The Christian must be reborn from above, converted by the Spirit. Jesus has come to restore the original truth of creation. He has come to give back to man the capacity and the courage of the destiny for which he was created. He is the true interpreter, greater than Moses, because He restores what was from the beginning. He is the fulfillment of the law, the One who does the Father's will, who lives every word that comes forth from the mouth of the Father. His heart is the realization of what was promised through Jeremiah and Ezekiel, in which the law of God is written. Thus, we return to *Veritatis Splendor*: "Only in the mystery of Christ's Redemption do we discover the 'concrete' possibilities of man."[15]

Today, it is often stated that what matters is not individual acts but charity or love. The fullness of Christian life is charity, the gift of oneself to God and one's neighbor; but love is rendered meaningless without truth or justice. It is reduced to a mere emotion rather than rooted in the good of the other. Thus, in speaking of the law of gradualness, we must acknowledge that with the initial conversion, there needs to be a minimal amount of love, namely in the repudiation of sin.

Only then can we begin to speak about growth in charity, through the consolidation and gradual perfection of one's own positive response to God. The negative precepts of the law indicate the minimum level, below which we have a contrast with the love of God. Charity necessarily demands respect for the minimal demands of the precepts of justice of the natural law. The positive precepts of the moral law and the counsels show, respectively, the ways of growth that are always ongoing and never concluded.

What, then, can we recommend? First, let us frankly acknowledge realities and difficulties, circumstances and existential realities. Second, let us have the courage to call things by their proper name. The first step for a journey is to identify the destination and the route by which one wants to arrive there. Third, we need to put in place those things necessary for a successful journey and to equip travelers for success. It is not enough to propose an ideal, to have good intentions; rather, it is important to have concrete strategies to arrive at the destination, learning from mistakes and sharing in the life of grace and redemption along the way.

We are thirty years removed from *Veritatis Splendor*, yet the task of the Church remains to help people to understand the greatness of the call to be a Christian and to assure them that they have a place in Christ's Church and that they will not be abandoned. At the same time, the Christian faithful need to be assured that they have trustworthy guides who are genuinely concerned about them and who will lead them by the light of truth along the path that leads to life—the fulfillment of their hearts' desires—and ultimately, to heaven.

Notes

1. John Paul II, *Veritatis Splendor* (1993), sec. 23.
2. *Veritatis Splendor*, sec. 119.
3. Benedict XVI, *Deus Caritas Est* (2005), sec. 1.
4. *Veritatis Splendor*, sec. 2.
5. *Veritatis Splendor*, sec. 7.
6. *Veritatis Splendor*, sec. 7.
7. *Veritatis Splendor*, sec. 106.
8. *Veritatis Splendor*, sec. 4.
9. *Veritatis Splendor*, sec. 46.
10. Francis, Address to a Decennial National Conference of the Italian Church (November 10, 2015).
11. *Veritatis Splendor*, sec. 7–8.
12. *Veritatis Splendor*, sec. 88.
13. *Veritatis Splendor*, sec. 53.
14. *Veritatis Splendor*, sec. 103.
15. *Veritatis Splendor*, sec. 103.

www.ingramcontent.com/pod-product-compliance
Lightning Source LLC
LaVergne TN
LVHW051601080426
835510LV00020B/3080